PRAISE F...
SAY THANK YOU FO...

"Gossipy, fun, insightful and simple—*Say Thank You For Everything* is the management book that works on great anecdotes, not tenuous metaphors. Enjoy these memorable examples of how to get it right at work and in life—as well as how to get it spectacularly wrong. So, Jim, as everyone is probably saying, thank you."

—Christian Broughton, managing director and former editor,
The Independent

"It's with great humor and humility that Jim Edwards teaches us not only how to be effective managers, but good business people. He walks us through all the emotions, the pitfalls, the lessons and the successes of being a boss. From expressing gratitude to admitting mistakes to reveling in each achievement, this is a perfect step-by-step guide for anyone just beginning their career in management. And it's a must-read for experienced managers who could use a swift kick in the pants. Everyone will come away with renewed energy and the skills to do their best."

—Michelle Gotthelf, former digital editor-in-chief
of *The New York Post*

"Most management advice books are incredibly boring. This one most definitely isn't. It's a great read for new managers."

—Donna Munday, executive producer,
Harry Potter and the Cursed Child

"*Say Thank You For Everything* is a deeply entertaining and educational look at leadership. The anecdotes gleaned from Edwards's 30-year career in media will make you laugh and gasp in horror, but at its heart this is a book about breaking the cycle of bad leadership. It's also an antidote to the 'cult of personality' model of being a boss; out with eccentric buffoonery, in with tangible takeaways to make you and your team better."

—Charlotte Owen, editor-in-chief, *Bustle*

"One of the big problems with leadership is that it's never taught. You do well as a contributor and then, if you're really good, you get promoted—as Jim did—to the confounding, uncomfortable and totally unfamiliar role of managing people. For those of us who've had that experience or ever hope to, *Say Thank You for Everything* is the manual we've been looking for. It's honest, approachable, free of jargon and full of practical advice. As I read it, I kept nodding in recognition. Jim knows how the leadership game is played and, better yet, he knows how to coach his readers to play it as well."

—Eric Schurenberg, CEO Mansueto Ventures
and former editor-in-chief of *Inc.* magazine

"As the original recipient of Jim's email that inspired this book, I can tell you first hand that his management advice is truly timeless. It has helped me time and again throughout my career. And true to Jim's own management style, this book is equal parts smart, funny, blunt and helpful."

—Alyson Shontell, editor-in-chief of *Fortune*

"We've all had bad managers. Some of them horrible. We've all had good managers. Some of them we love as if they were family. (And honestly we might prefer them.) But what truly separates the good from the bad, the beloved from the atrocious? Never has a book answered that very question—until now. With his signature wisdom and wit, Jim Edwards has created the ultimate instruction manual for how to manage, lead, and inspire a team—and how not to fuck it up along the way. This is officially now required reading for all current or aspiring bosses."

—Kathryn Tuggle, editor-in-chief of *HerMoney*
and co-author of *How To Money*

SAY
THANK YOU
FOR
EVERYTHING

Every owner of a physical copy of this edition of

SAY THANK YOU FOR EVERYTHING

can download the eBook for free direct from us at Harriman House, in a DRM-free format that can be read on any eReader, tablet or smartphone.

Simply head to:

ebooks.harriman-house.com/ saythankyouforeverything

to get your copy now.

SAY
THANK YOU
FOR
EVERYTHING

THE SECRETS OF BEING
A GREAT MANAGER

STRATEGIES AND TACTICS
THAT GET RESULTS

JIM EDWARDS

HARRIMAN HOUSE LTD
3 Viceroy Court
Bedford Road
Petersfield
Hampshire
GU32 3LJ
GREAT BRITAIN
Tel: +44 (0)1730 233870

Email: enquiries@harriman-house.com
Website: harriman.house

First published in 2022.
Copyright © Jim Edwards

The right of Jim Edwards to be identified as the Author has been asserted in accordance with the Copyright, Design and Patents Act 1988.

Paperback ISBN: 978-0-85719-934-8
eBook ISBN: 978-0-85719-935-5

British Library Cataloguing in Publication Data
A CIP catalogue record for this book can be obtained from the British Library.

For Philippa

CONTENTS

III. PEOPLE   91

IV. DECISIONS   197

INTRODUCTION

The boss who bit people

THERE is a reason *The Devil Wears Prada* is set in the media business and not, say, at a charity for rescuing orphans. The film is based on a book written by Lauren Weisberger, a former assistant to Anna Wintour, the legendary editor-in-chief of *Vogue*. It depicts a fictional Wintour, named Miranda Priestly, as a despotic sociopath who psychologically tortures the assistants who work at her fashion magazine.

Although the movie shows an exaggerated version of Wintour—aloof, demanding, fickle—it is nonetheless based on real life. Wintour once suggested to Oprah Winfrey that she should lose some weight, for instance. Assistants to Anna Wintour have hung her coats up for her as if they were her butlers. They have carried her bags. They have been advised not to engage in eye contact. They have been asked to perform demeaning personal chores such as fetching her dry cleaning, according to André Leon Talley, a former editor at *Vogue* who worked alongside Wintour for 27 years.

Anyone who has worked in the media in real life has come across a boss like Priestly or Wintour. Real-life media bosses are sometimes worse than their Hollywood counterparts.

I once worked for Steve Brill, the fearsome author and

founder of Court TV, American Lawyer, NewsGuard, and other businesses. He behaved like a demanding boss from central casting. He lit cigars in the office even though everyone else was banned from smoking in the building. He wore suspender-braces instead of a belt. He yelled at people he didn't like. I once made a printout of a story I was working on and accidentally left it in the reception area near his office. It was a rough draft and I was nowhere near finished with it. Brill found it and emailed the entire company with a detailed critique of everything he didn't like about my writing. It was humiliating.

But I got off lightly.

Brill once allegedly bit—with his teeth—one of his own employees. The victim was Jim Cramer, who later became a famous hedge fund manager and the host of the *Mad Money* show on CNBC. Yes, Steve Brill *bit* Jim Cramer.

It happened at a company party Brill hosted at his mansion in Westchester, New York. Brill had a swimming pool at his house and pitted his employees against each other in a game of water polo. The game quickly got out of hand, because Brill hated losing.

"Just as I was about to score what would have been the tying goal for my team, Brill sank his teeth into my throwing arm, spouting blood into the clear water in a steady stream. As everyone looked on in horror, I could only laugh. That was Steve all over," Cramer later wrote in his autobiography.

Don't feel sorry for Cramer, by the way.

As a boss, Cramer was equally terrible on his worst days. In his hedge fund office, Cramer's rage controlled him. He smashed fax machines. He railed at construction workers in the street outside. He even hated the birds on his windowsill. His psychiatrist tried to prescribe him drugs to calm him down—and Cramer screamed his refusal.

On one occasion, "He started smashing his phone over and over on the desk in front of him. He lifted a monitor and heaved it like a shot put. After several feet, it shattered on the floor," according to Nicholas Maier, who worked with him at the hedge fund. Maier was so disturbed by Cramer's behavior that he wrote a whole book about it, called *Trading With the Enemy*.

The Hollywood model of a bad boss is something that many bad bosses buy into. I have seen them screaming at their colleagues. I have received their ALL-CAPS tantrums in office-wide emails. I have read their handwritten notes—battlefields of red ink.

There is one good thing about having a bad boss. It teaches you not to be like that. Everyone has a war story about an awful former boss. A significant part of most companies' management training consists of workers mentally resolving that they will never treat their colleagues this way. If you think being a manager means behaving like Brill or Cramer or Wintour or Priestly, then you are in for a shock. No decent company works like this anymore. (And if you are in a company that works like this, leave immediately.)

WHY THIS BOOK EXISTS

Learning from war stories about bad bosses is entertaining, no doubt, but what you really need is some basic common-sense advice on how not to be the worst manager on the planet. The good news? It's not terrifically complicated. Anyone can become a good boss if they are willing to put in the work.

I wrote this book because I learned a lot from the unique management culture of Insider Inc., the news media company that is best known for creating *Business Insider*.

Business Insider was originally a blog, started by four people in 2007. They worked in a tiny office in a third-floor walkup at 134 Fifth Avenue in Manhattan. In reality, the office was a loading dock where FedEx deliveries were received for another company. When the FedEx drivers came, the Insider team had to get up and move their chairs to let them in. In its first few years of existence, quite a lot of people predicted that Insider would go bankrupt.

Today, Insider reaches up to 200 million readers per month. It generates more than $150 million in sales annually. Eight years after it was launched, it was sold at a valuation of $442m to Axel Springer, the German publishing giant. The company is worth much more than that today.

Insider is successful in large part because its internal culture is very different from its competitors'.

I have also learned a lot from my mistakes. I have learned what not to do. I am also, as this book will make clear, not the best manager who ever walked the earth. Far from it. The good news about that is, you don't have to be the best manager in order to be a good one—someone who is effective and who outperforms their peers and competitors.

This book is *not* an official account of Insider's internal management practices, although obviously I have been influenced by them. It is based on my own career, spanning more than 20 years working for over a dozen companies. I have worked for CBS News, *Slate*, *Salon*, *The Independent*, MTV, *The Nation*, AOL, *Adweek*, *Brill's Content*, APBnews, *The New Jersey Law Journal* and two daily newspapers: *The Herald & News* of North Jersey and *The Register Citizen* of Connecticut.

I have been managing teams of various sizes since the mid-1990s. Some teams were small: just three people including myself. When I wrote this book, I managed Insider's News division, which had 80 people scattered between London, New York, California, and Singapore. Insider employed about 600 journalists globally and more than 900 employees in total at the time of writing, and I was on the company's executive committee, which broadly supervises all of them.

Surprisingly, the things you need to know to make a small team run smoothly have a lot in common with making a big team successful.

WOULD YOU LIKE SOME UNSOLICITED ADVICE?

The original inspiration for this book came in August 2016, when a friend received a huge promotion, placing her in charge of a team of nearly 100 people. I picked up the phone to congratulate her on the opportunity of a lifetime. She told me she was elated but also terrified that she was in over her head.

When I got back to my desk I thought it might be a nice gesture to send her a note; just a few tips I had learned over the years. No big deal. The email I eventually sent was titled, sarcastically, "Would you like some unsolicited advice?" It contained a list of 19 tricks that, over the years, had made my life easier as a manager.

Since then, every time someone I know is promoted to supervise others, I send them a copy of that email. It doesn't matter how big their team is—one person or 100—they get the same email. Nineteen pieces of unsolicited advice. Dozens of my friends and colleagues have received this email.

The email has barely changed over the years. The 19 pieces of advice work well no matter who receives them. As long as they are supervising someone, the email is useful. The very final piece of advice in the email is this:

> Say "thank you" for everything. Literally thank people all the time for the work they do, the time they put in. Tell them you appreciate it. You can defuse virtually any job stress among staff by saying "Thank you for doing that, I really appreciate it, it was a lot of work and it did not go unnoticed. Great job."

Many of the chapters in *Say Thank You for Everything* are expanded directly from the original 19 pieces of unsolicited advice in that email. But that last notion—the mere act of showing gratitude to your colleagues—is the starting point of this book.

WHO THIS BOOK IS FOR

This book is for anyone in an industry that requires the slightest amount of creativity: media, marketing, advertising, sales, PR, project management, software engineering, tech startups, politics, charities and nonprofits—you name it. It is for anyone in a results-oriented industry, like retail, food, restaurants, or manufacturing. It is for anyone working in an environment where you supervise a team and are judged on their results.

It is intended to be a short and easy-to-read book of advice containing everything you need to know about managing a team. It is aimed primarily at newly promoted supervisors who have never been anyone's boss before, or people who suddenly find themselves supervising much larger groups than they are used to. It contains advice that should be helpful all the way up to CEO level.

HOW THIS BOOK IS ORGANIZED

I have organized this book in the hope that it best fits your needs as a new manager. Maybe you have never supervised people before and this is your first promotion. Perhaps you have been managing people for a while but have never received any formal management training—and now realize, wisely, that it is time you got some. Or maybe your career is advanced and, like the original recipient of my email, you now have to tackle the biggest leadership challenge of your career. This book contains advice that should, in principle, work in any situation.

It starts with the simple stuff—the basic things you need to know immediately. For instance, the best way to approach Day One of your new job.

Then it works its way through some of the more complicated,

in-depth problems you're likely to encounter as you gain more experience. Improving the performance of a team takes time, for example, and there is a series of chapters on how to do that.

The final few chapters deal with bigger, heavier, more conceptual issues, such as using data to solve strategic problems that might affect the whole company.

HOW TO READ THIS BOOK

I am very influenced by Axios, the online news service, which has adopted a specific writing style its editors call "smart brevity." The Axios style utilizes a lot of sub-headlines, bullet points, and lists. Its articles are often not written as stories in a traditional narrative format but as collections of related points presented in a logical order. They are also usually short.

The purpose of smart brevity is to save readers as much time as possible while delivering as much information as possible. Likewise, this book contains lots of short chapters, subheads, and lists. They are intended to give you many different entry points if you only want to dip in and out of it.

And you don't have to read the whole thing from beginning to end if you don't feel like it. If you are pressed for time (or simply cannot be bothered!), the end of every chapter sums up its practical advice in a series of ten-second cheat sheets.

The chapters are organized into four overarching themes to help you find relevant clusters of content and move about the book more nimbly. Don't feel restricted by them.

HERE IS WHAT YOU WILL *NOT* FIND
INSIDE THESE PAGES

Most management advice books are long and boring. I have deliberately tried to keep this short. It contains a ton of hands-on, day-to-day advice.

This book is intended to be practical rather than inspirational:

- This is not a book about the mythic qualities of leadership, although it will help you be a better leader.
- This is not a self-help book about personal success, although it will help you be more successful.
- It's not about product building, startup launching, value creation, or any of those "inspirational business book" things.

This book is about one simple thing: How to manage people so that your teams become more successful, as quickly and efficiently as possible, while not being an ass about it. Especially if you have never done it before.

Thank you for reading this book.

DISCLOSURE

All the stories I tell in this book are true. To be clear, many of them did not happen at Insider. Many of them are from earlier points in my career. Some were told to me by friends, and happened at places I did not work but where I knew people who did. Because the anecdotes often involve people making terrible errors, I have changed various details—names, places, and times—to protect the reputations of former colleagues whose careers should not be remembered solely for their worst-ever day at the office.

I
LEADERSHIP

1

LEADERSHIP

1

Day One: What the fuck is going on?

CONGRATULATIONS! You have a new job as a manager. It's your first day on the job. Day One.

What is the first thing you should do?

Being appointed as a manager will often be a battlefield promotion. Good companies are almost always extremely busy places. There is a lot going on. It's a frenzy. Competition is fierce. Suddenly, someone leaves! And then the boss turns to you: "Are you willing to step up and run this team?"

It means more money and a fancier job title. Obviously, you say *yes*.

There is a good chance that when you are promoted, you will be dumped straight in the deep end. You will be expected to run your team from Day One. There will be no honeymoon period.

Work needs to be finished today. People need to be organized, deadlines met, sales made. If you are a new manager, you will need a plan immediately.

What follows is a good example of how to approach Day One.

IN THE SAME ROOM BUT NOT ON THE SAME PAGE

Several years ago, a friend joined an obscure tech startup which was developing an app that linked social media users to news content. (I am not going to name the company, in order to spare the blushes of those involved.) It was a small firm in San Francisco, which had perhaps 50 other employees grouped into teams of three to six people. They all sat together on the same floor, Bloomberg style—meaning it was an open-plan office where everyone sat at equally sized desks. No one sat inside an office with a door that closed. Everyone could see or hear what everyone else was doing.

One team was larger than the others: it had eight people, and it was run by a guy I'll call Paul. Everyone thought Paul's team was the most successful in the company. They were the heartbeat of the firm. They created the most new features on the app, and those features attracted the most new users. They epitomized its best people. Paul's team was the largest, made the most noise, and got the most attention from the CEO. They were setting the pace. You could tell that by the volume of their banter.

My friend—let's call her Kathryn—was working in one of the company's smallest and most obscure teams. They only had three people, including Kathryn. Their desks were against the wall, in the far corner of the office—as far from the center of the action as could be. They got very little attention from management or from their colleagues.

After a few months, the CEO came to Kathryn and asked her to take over the leadership of Paul's team. Paul was moving on to a different project.

Of course, she said *yes*. It was a big move up.

However, what the CEO had not told Kathryn was that he had deliberately not promoted someone from within Paul's team. He wanted an outsider in charge.

It was only after Kathryn took over Paul's team that she got a look at what was really going on, from the inside. Sure, the team had some good performers doing high-profile work. But their results had been in decline for weeks. They weren't shipping enough product. The team was flailing. None of their colleagues outside the team knew this yet, because their reputation was so good.

Kathryn had *not* been promoted to build on their success.

She had been promoted to *rescue* them.

Her first problem was to figure out why the best unit of the company had gone adrift. So Kathryn began interviewing each member of staff individually. She booked 30 minutes with each of them. Sometimes they went to Starbucks to talk in private. Other times they hunkered down on a sofa in the reception area at the front of the office, away from everyone else's desks.

The first person Kathryn interviewed was Dave.

She asked to talk to Dave first because Dave's desk was face to face with Paul's. Dave was the person who worked physically closest to Paul. He could hear all of Paul's phone calls and see all of his desk-side conversations. He would know where the bodies were buried. Surely, Dave would be able to get Kathryn up to speed quickly.

They began talking. "How's it going?" Kathryn asked him.

"I just want to know what the fuck is going on," Dave said.

"What do you mean?"

"I mean literally. I have no idea what's going on. No one tells me anything. What's the big picture? What are we supposed to be aiming for? I'm working in the dark."

"You sat opposite Paul," Kathryn said. "How can you not know what's going on?"

"He didn't tell me anything," Dave said.

Kathryn was floored.

It didn't seem possible that someone could sit right next to his boss, every day, and not know what the company's plan was.

BENIGN ANARCHY DOESN'T WORK

As Kathryn interviewed the rest of the team, it turned out that Dave wasn't alone. The team was internally disorganized. They didn't have a weekly meeting with each other. Paul had not set deadlines or goals for the team to meet. They didn't share a team calendar so that people could see the events that others were working towards. Some of them worked on their own and had no involvement with the rest of the team. Others worked in pairs. Paul had never communicated a long-term vision. Instead, he issued instructions on the fly, off the top of his head. His days were one long, random conversation with his staff, without structure.

Paul had run his team like a benign anarchist. When the team was smaller, it had worked well. Paul's team had been successful when it was just four or five people including Paul himself. That success had encouraged the CEO to add members to his team. But after the team grew to eight people, things started falling apart.

Paul let his staff do what they wanted and hoped for the best. Now the atmosphere inside the team was chaotic.

Why did this go wrong?

THE RULE OF FIVE

The answer to this question has been known for over a century. Back in 1913 a French agricultural engineer named Maximilien Ringelmann published a research paper that described a curious phenomenon: when he asked farm workers to pull on a rope to produce the maximum force possible over an extended period, folks exerted less effort when they pulled as part of a team than they did as individuals. As a rule of thumb, the more people you add to a rope-pulling team, the less force each team member exerts on the rope. Ringelmann theorized that as more people were added to the team, interpersonal communication between team members became a distraction from the goal, reducing the team's total effectiveness.

Since then, the Ringelmann effect has been reproduced by dozens of other social scientists trying to explain why teams lose motivation and coordination as they get bigger.

In a very small team—two or three people—communication isn't a big deal. It's obvious what the manager of the team wants, and instructions can be communicated in a series of ongoing personal conversations. It's easy to stay on the same wavelength with two other people, after all. There is hardly any chance of a misunderstanding. You can easily talk to everyone else on the team very quickly.

However, once a team grows above five people, problems start to kick in.

In 1972 the University of Massachusetts psychologist Ivan D. Steiner discovered that adding a sixth person to a team reduces its effectiveness, and team performance actually gets worse as you add more people. At Harvard in the 1970s, J. Richard Hackman, a psychology professor, banned his students from organizing themselves into study groups of more than six people. He published research that suggested the optimal team size is 4.6 people.

That 4.6 statistic has become a management psychology legend over the years. Both *Fortune* and *Forbes* magazines have since reported that 4.6 is the optimum number of people for a productive work team. (Of course, to reach that optimum you'd have to slice someone into pieces. Oddly, no researchers have addressed this in their articles.)

Five is therefore the crucial threshold. Anything up to five is optimal. Once you hit six, you are flirting with the threshold of dysfunction.

You have probably noticed this phenomenon yourself. If you are at a dinner party for four people, everyone talks as a group and everyone is included in the same conversation. Anyone who is not talking can hear everyone else clearly. But once you have six or more guests at a table, you're likely to find yourselves dividing into smaller, separate conversations in groups of three or four. At a dinner party for eight, guests at opposite ends of the table will have had completely different experiences of the meal, even though they are sitting just a few feet away from each other.

This was Paul's problem: he was hosting a dinner party for eight, but he was still behaving as if there were only four guests at the table.

THE TWO QUESTIONS ALL NEW MANAGERS SHOULD ASK ON DAY ONE

The other problem Kathryn had was that the members of Paul's team were all more experienced in the business than she was. Kathryn had been asked to supervise a team where she was, technically, the least-knowledgeable member. This was awkward. They had no reason to respect her. In fact, they had good reason to resent her: her appointment as their boss meant that none of them had been offered the promotion.

Ignoring that issue would have been ridiculous. Honesty is usually the best policy, so Kathryn decided to face this head-on. In her conversation with Dave she said, "Look, everyone on this team knows more about this business than me, so I have decided to ask everyone's advice before I start ordering people around. Tell me: What is working well? What should we do more of?"

Dave responded, and then she asked him the opposite. "What is the team doing wrong? What's failing? What should we stop doing?"

His answers to those questions were even more revealing.

Kathryn took notes as he talked, and told him she would use

his advice in a new plan she was making for the whole team, in hopes of getting them back on track.

You should ask those same questions of every member of the team you supervise. These are the two most valuable questions you can ask of anyone in any organization:

1. What works?
2. What does not?

Almost anything can be improved by doing more of the tasks that are really productive and by dropping the work that just isn't going anywhere.

TURN *THEIR* PLAN INTO *YOUR* PLAN

The answers you get to those two questions will be some of the most useful information you will ever receive. Rank-and-file employees almost always know how to do the work quicker, more efficiently, more productively, than anyone else. They know what little things a company might do to save money. But these secrets, these valuable efficiencies, remain locked away until someone from management bothers to ask them. Make it your job to ask them.

By the end of the first day, you will emerge with some major advantages as the new boss:

- Your people feel they are being listened to, which is hugely important.
- Your people feel they are influencing your plan for their future. (And you will more easily get their buy-in.)
- You get the benefit of all their good ideas, which you can then turn into a usable plan that will get measurable improvements from your team. You get a ton of actionable

information just by asking everyone else what you should do. And that will help you overcome your inexperience.

I am not saying you should do every single thing they tell you. That would be ridiculous. You're the boss—so you need to use your judgment about what can and cannot be done.

In the case of Paul's old team, what they needed most was organization.

Kathryn set up a weekly meeting where they brainstormed new ideas and generated new projects to tackle. She measured their performance consistently, every month, so everyone knew where they stood and how far they had to go. And she bombarded them with team emails so that everyone got the same message at the same time, and there was no confusion. (Yes, I know everyone hates work emails, but sometimes you have to!) It took a couple of months, but their results improved and the team got back on track.

TEN-SECOND CHEAT SHEET

- ⊘ Set up an individual meeting with every member of your new staff.

- ⊘ Ask them what is working well; what should the company do more of?

- ⊘ Ask them what is failing; what should you drop?

- ⊘ Tell them you will use their advice in a new plan for the team.

- ⊘ Turn their plan into your plan.

- ⊘ Increase the amount of communication they get, whether that is face to face with you, via emails, or in team meetings.

⌚ Remember the rule of five: If you can group the people you supervise into separate teams of five people or fewer, do it.

⌚ If you can group them into threes, even better. Threes work really well.

⌚ Take your team to lunch on your first day as their new manager. It helps build relationships and smooth wrinkles between staff.

2

America's worst-ever pizza restaurant as a model of good leadership

Oᴎᴇ of the most difficult aspects of management is providing leadership. Most people do not regard themselves as natural leaders. Yet even if you are supervising just one other person's work, you will need to show leadership (whatever that is).

Leadership is a mushy concept. It implies you have to be an inspiring, legendary figure. A war general. A preacher. A soothsayer. Impossibly brave or impossibly eloquent, like Churchill or Kennedy or the activist Tarana Burke or the author Elif Shafak.

In the movies, when Hollywood creates an inspiring boss scene, you'll see that boss stand on a desk to give a speech. Everyone cheers! People pump their fists in the air! Delirious listeners throw things above their heads in celebration!

This does not happen in real life.

There is a performative side to leadership, certainly, but I would caution you about overdoing it. Your staff probably don't want to see you standing on a soapbox every day yelling, "Go team!"

Instead, think about Patrick Doyle, the former president of the Domino's pizza chain.

"WORST PIZZA I EVER HAD"

In late 2009 a series of previously confidential videos filmed by the Domino's pizza chain made their way onto YouTube. The videos depicted the company's internal focus groups, which Domino's used to monitor how consumers felt about their products. Focus group recordings are typically made with a camera hidden on the other side of a two-way mirror. They take place inside windowless rooms, so that no one can hear what is going on. They remain closely guarded corporate secrets.

These video sessions were brutal. Consumers *hated* Domino's pizza. In one video a woman said, "Domino's pizza crust to me is like cardboard." Another added, "The sauce tastes like ketchup." "Worst pizza I ever had," said a third.

One of the focus group attendees, a woman identified only as Adrienne, subjected Domino's staff to a little speech in which she questioned whether Domino's even understood what pizza is. In the video, her face bore an expression of bemused anger. "Pizza? Where's the love?" she said. "Bread, sauce, cheese, fresh ingredients. Doesn't feel like there's much love in Domino's pizza."

Domino's senior leadership watched the videos in dismay.

Marketing director Karen Kaiser reviewed some of the notes from the sessions. "This one is bad: 'Worst excuse for pizza I've ever had,'" she said.

Looking at the videos, product manager Meredith Baker almost choked up. "It's hard to watch," she said. Consumers liked almost nothing about Domino's pizza. Not the sauce. Not the cheese. Not the bread. The crust quality came up repeatedly.

"The 'cardboard' complaint is the most common one," Phil Lozen, a Domino's PR executive, said gloomily.

The videos merely confirmed the trouble that Domino's management already knew it was in. Sales were in heavy decline. The company had lost 15% of its revenues in the prior two years.

Domino's, and its 9,000 franchise restaurants worldwide, were slowly imploding.

So president Patrick Doyle decided to do something about it. Printouts of customers' negative reviews were posted all around the offices in Ann Arbor, Michigan, so that no employee could be under any illusions. "Boring, artificial imitation of what pizza can be," said one note. "Crust seemed lacking," read another.

Doyle asked his corporate chefs to remake the company's core product from scratch. The executive kitchen staff tried ten new crust types. They created 15 different sauces. They reviewed dozens of new cheeses before they got it right. "They were working day and night and weekends to get it done," Doyle said.

The reason we know all this is that in early 2010 Domino's relaunched its pizza and turned the awful internal videos into an ad campaign. They promoted their former failings. Like a recovering alcoholic hitting rock bottom, Domino's asked for forgiveness, to be given a second chance.

It worked.

People were charmed by Domino's honesty. Sales rebounded by 16.5% almost immediately. With the new growth, Domino's stock exploded upward. For the prior two years, Domino's shares had been worth less than $10 each. Suddenly, they doubled in price. Then tripled. Then tripled again. At the time of writing, Domino's stock traded for $530 per share.

"THIS IS NOT ACCEPTABLE"

Domino's pizza turnaround campaign is one of the boldest and most unusual product relaunches in history. It may be unique.

It was also a logistical nightmare. All the ingredients changed, which meant all the supplies had to change. The recipe changed, which meant all 9,000 Domino's franchise locations had to learn new instructions for cooking the new recipe. After the pizza launched, Domino's went on to redesign every single delivery box. Domino's employed about 180,000 people at the time of the turnaround. Every single one of them, at some point, was asked to do something new and different to make the plan work.

But they didn't stop there. A later video published by the company shows Doyle holding a framed photo of an appalling pizza sent in by an unhappy customer. The lid of the delivery box has been squashed flat onto the pie itself, rendering it inedible. Doyle makes a solemn vow to the camera. "This is not acceptable. Bryce in Minnesota, you shouldn't have to get this from Domino's, we're better than this."

The company's ongoing ad campaign then showed Domino's staff tracking down unhappy customers, including Bryce—people who had written scathing online reviews. One video showed a Domino's team stalking a former customer named Bill Johnson to his house. They plastered his neighborhood with flyers that said, "Bill Johnson, you'll love our new cheese!" Besieged, he eventually relented, opened his front door, and ate a free slice of the new pizza on his doorstep. Of course, he loved it.

The campaign was designed by Crispin Porter + Bogusky, an ad agency known for its off-the-wall ideas. You can dismiss all this as clever marketing, but that would be missing the point: A large part of being in business involves clever marketing. Being clever at marketing is a valuable skill. And what was being marketed was real: Domino's executives really did admit their pizza was garbage. They really did ditch everything and start again from scratch. "We basically had to start over to get it right," Kaiser, the marketing director, said.

But the real joy of the campaign is watching the Domino's staff defend and advance their new product. With the pizza fixed, they're raring to get out there and introduce it to the world.

The Domino's story encapsulates several qualities you want to see in good leadership. It's worth boiling down Domino's plan to its basics, because it is a great example of what good leadership looks like at a company that needs to change:

- Management admitted it had a serious problem and that doing nothing was not an option. There was no "just hoping" things might get better on their own.
- They were open and transparent with their own staff, and the public, about how bad the problem was. They didn't try to cover it up with PR spin.
- They came up with a plan to fix the problem. The plan was clear, bold, and easily understood.
- Management was transparent about the amount of extra work the turnaround would create. People worked nights and weekends. They rebuilt the product from scratch.
- They had faith in Domino's staff having enough talent and ability to improve the product. They gave them the creative freedom to completely rebuild the core product.
- They took a huge risk: Domino's didn't know that people would like their new pizza. They couldn't force people to try it or to forgive them once it was available.
- Management stood up for the work, and by implication the staff who did that work. They defended the company and its product against critics. It is important for staff to see that their bosses have their backs. Doyle probably did more media interviews in 2010 than any other CEO on the planet.
- There was an important strategic purpose: Doyle, the president, turned the company's biggest disadvantage—its terrible reputation—into its chief asset.
- Although the videos were no doubt initially embarrassing for the company, they drew a line under the old Domino's and thereby confined the problem to the past. The company

was no longer held back by its historic baggage. Going forward, it was a new company making a fresh start.

Nothing Doyle said was particularly inspiring. He isn't a great performer. He doesn't look mercurial. He wasn't projecting power. He didn't walk onto a stage wearing a black turtleneck sweater, like Apple's Steve Jobs delivering his legendary "one more thing" keynotes. He didn't do a TED Talk. In the videos, Doyle wears a polo shirt rather than a designer suit or a silk tie. He looks like the person in the office cubicle next to you, not one of Tom Wolfe's Masters of the Universe. If he lived next door to you, you would not notice him.

But Doyle had a great plan. He laid it out clearly. He didn't bullshit his people. He set a clear goal for the entire company. And he stood up for the work. This is what good leadership looks like. Anyone can do it.

You can do it.

TEN-SECOND CHEAT SHEET

- Don't worry about being a leader. Leadership is a set of practices. It is not a mystical aura that you summon through the sheer force of your personality.

- Don't bullshit your staff. Workers want their bosses to be honest and clear about the task in front of them. Be transparent.

- They want to know that you have a plan, they want to know what the plan is, and they want you to organize that plan so they can complete their tasks meaningfully and productively within it.

- ⌚ Don't procrastinate. Staff need you to make decisions. Especially *difficult* decisions. The faster you can make decisions, the better. Refusing to make decisions—or just being really slow to react—is an especially good way to become a terrible boss.

- ⌚ Good leaders change tactics and strategies quickly when the market or the environment moves against them. Choose to change now—or have change forced upon you by your enemies.

- ⌚ Stand up for the work your people do. Be seen to be standing up for it. Believe in it. Advocate for it.

- ⌚ Give your staff as much freedom to solve problems, generate solutions, and come up with new ideas as you possibly can. (Within reasonable limits, of course—you're running a business, not an artists' colony!)

- ⌚ Fake it till you make it. Remember, no one else in management knows what they're doing either. Just do your best and act like that's normal.

3

Change is better than standing in the dust at the side of the road saying, "But we have always done it this way!"

THE Domino's story is a remarkably clear example of how difficult it can be for you, the new boss, to ask a team of people to start doing something differently. Changing the pizza was essentially an indictment of everything that everyone at the company had been doing for the previous three decades. When Domino's management said to their staff, "We need new pizza," it was the equivalent of saying to all their workers, "You are terrible at making pizza."

Your problem, as a manager, is that you will frequently be asking your people to change—and that can be really tough. You may be saying, "Please do this new thing," but what many workers hear is, "I do not care that you worked really hard on the old thing."

"This new thing isn't what I signed up for," they might respond. "I have done everything you have asked me to do. What's the problem?"

People can get really angry and frustrated about this. As their manager, you are going to be the target of much of that. It will not be fun. In my experience, there is no easy way to tell a member of staff, or a team, or a whole company, "You need to change." You just have to be straightforward and honest about it.

You might also discuss with them the price of *not* changing.

BLOCKBUSTER SUCCUMBED TO ITS OWN STUBBORNNESS

There are a lot of inspirational innovation stories in the business press about how such-and-such a genius invented a new thing and now the whole world is different! But what happened to all the people who did not change quickly enough—the people who failed?

My favorite example of failing to change involves the Blockbuster video rental chain, which most people think was forced out of business by the internet. This is not what happened. Blockbuster succumbed to its own stubbornness.

In 2000 Blockbuster dominated the movie rental business. If you wanted to watch a film of your choice in the evening, there was only one way to do it: Drive to your local Blockbuster and rent a physical DVD or VHS tape. At its peak, Blockbuster had about 80,000 employees and 9,000 stores worldwide. Its stock market value was more than $5 billion. For the previous decade just about every man, woman, and child in the US and the UK watched a movie from Blockbuster. Remembering to return the Blockbuster video on Monday morning was a ubiquitous weekly chore.

This is where your mental narrator voice might jump in to intone: "But the internet was about to change everything!"

Incorrect.

The internet was not in fact changing everything for Blockbuster in the year 2000. At that time, the web was still in its infancy. Most web users got their access via dial-up phone lines, which were not fast enough to handle movies. A huge percentage of the population had no internet access at all. And no one owned a mobile phone capable of playing a watchable video.

In that year Netflix, like Blockbuster, was only a physical video rental service. Neither company offered an internet service. The only difference between the two was that Netflix let you order and return DVDs through the postal service, for longer time periods, whereas Blockbuster required you to go to its stores. Legend has it that founder Reed Hastings got the idea for Netflix in the late 1990s when he returned an overdue Blockbuster video and was annoyed by the large penalty fee.

By 2000, however, Hastings was desperate, according to his book, *No Rules Rules*. Netflix was hemorrhaging money. He didn't believe the company would survive. So he begged for a meeting at Blockbuster's corporate headquarters in Dallas with CEO John Antioco. In the meeting, he offered to sell Netflix to Blockbuster for $50m, a trivial sum for a company of Blockbuster's size. In return, Hastings would come aboard to develop Blockbuster.com as a new online video-renting service. The internet was not currently good enough for video, but it soon would be, he argued.

Antioco said *no*.

Netflix did not launch its online streaming service until seven years *after* this fateful meeting. Blockbuster had all that time to figure out its online strategy, but didn't. Netflix successfully made the jump from physical DVDs to online streaming in 2007. The internet, eventually, turned out to be a better way to watch a film than driving back and forth to a store. At the time of writing, Netflix is worth $300bn. Blockbuster went bankrupt in 2010.

Blockbuster was sunk by its stubbornness and not by the internet. The proof? Netflix wasn't the only company Blockbuster passed on. In the early 1990s, the cable and satellite TV companies began offering a rich selection of video-on-demand choices via the high-speed lines they already had running into set-top boxes in millions of homes. Time Warner, AT&T, DirecTV, and half a dozen others all saw that the ability to deliver a movie without the viewer having to leave the sofa was a winning formula. Blockbuster considered buying one of these companies in about 1993... but didn't go through with the idea. It doubled down on its stores instead. In other words, Blockbuster whiffed on two different waves of incoming change.

Today, streaming video services collectively generate nearly $90bn in sales every year. There are dozens of them. Netflix is a famous one, but it is far from dominant globally. Had Blockbuster bought *any* cable or internet video service between 1993 and 2007—14 years!—it might have survived.

Like I said, this was about stubbornness, not the internet changing everything.

SUCCESS ISN'T DELIVERED BY ELVES IN THE NIGHT

It's worth describing the big picture so that staff understand the nature of the business you are in and what is at stake if they cannot change: success doesn't magically appear on its own. It isn't delivered by elves in the night. It requires hard work and experimentation.

It is very, very common for people to believe their work is good simply because they did it. A lot of people genuinely believe that their work has an inherent value. It *must* do, if the company is paying them to do it, right? It can be difficult for professionals to admit that they have worked for an extended period of time on a project that is yielding paltry results.

A team or a company can lose its way pretty quickly if everyone is just trying to do their job and resists new initiatives. When people do the same thing, over and over, every day, without change, sclerosis and inertia set in. The competitive health of a company can be judged by how quickly it is able to execute something new. After all, organizations are not islands. They are surrounded by competitors. A company that is resistant to change is a company that will quickly be threatened by rivals for which change is an opportunity.

Change is tough. It's inconvenient. It's hard work, and it requires you to admit that you were failing at the old thing and now need to do a new thing. None of that feels good. But change is better than the alternative—which is unemployment.

So it is worth telling skeptical colleagues the truth. Everything changes, and so must they.

- Technology changes.
- The market changes.
- Customers change.
- Competitors change.
- The companies you're in partnership with—suppliers, contractors—change.

You don't want to end up standing in the dust at the side of the road, holding a Blockbuster DVD, insisting that everything will be OK because "We have always done it this way!"

Change can be hard and it's reasonable that it makes some employees nervous. You need to be gentle but firm. But, eventually, you should be upfront with your staff: Freaking out whenever something changes is not helpful. It doesn't help you deal with change. It doesn't help the company deal with change. And while change is a pain in the backside, it is better than the alternative: Blockbuster video.

OF COURSE, NOT EVERYONE RESISTS CHANGE

In reality, some staff love change. Change brings new opportunities and the chance to learn new skills. For every Domino's pizza chef whose heart was broken during the turnaround, there were probably a dozen or more staffers who thanked the heavens that they were finally making something that didn't look and taste like crap. For every Blockbuster employee who lost a job renting DVDs, ten new jobs have opened at companies like Netflix, Amazon and HBO developing software and creating new shows for online video streaming companies.

Lean into this. Encourage these members of staff. These are the people who get it; the people who are excited to see what is around the next corner. The builders and the crankers—the people who want to create something new and are willing to work hard to get there—will embrace change.

These are the people you need.

TEN-SECOND CHEAT SHEET

⌚ It is easy to ask people to change the work they do, but change is often logistically difficult.

⌚ When you ask staff to enact changes at work, you may say, "Please do this new thing," but what many workers will hear is, "I do not care that you worked really hard on the old thing." Staff can get angry and frustrated when asked to change.

⌚ There is little you can do about this, except to clearly repeat the logic of the change and lay out the plan ahead, as Domino's did. As time passes, resistance will wane.

⌚ You have to be straightforward and honest with your staff about what change will entail. It's worth describing the big picture, so that staff understand the nature of the business you are in and what is at stake.

⌚ Tell staff the truth: Freaking out about change is not helpful. It doesn't help you deal with change. It doesn't help the company deal with change.

⌚ Change is a pain in the ass but it is better than the alternative: unemployment.

4

The war against mushroom farming: How to communicate effectively

WHEN I first joined Insider, the first team I supervised consisted of just three people: Me as the editor, and two reporters. Running a team of three was easy. We all sat next to each other. We talked to each other across our desks. I didn't think much about communication because we had no communication problems. As such, we took change in our stride. If something new needed to be done, we just did it. Life in a small team is like this: Change is easy because communication is easy.

When I moved from New York to London to start up the UK operation of Insider, I quickly hired about 12 people to work with me.

And then a funny thing happened. I would ask for a task to be done—something simple, like, "Please make sure the front page of the website is updated at noon!"—and it wouldn't get done.

So the next day I asked again: "Please change the front page at noon every day!"

Didn't happen.

On day three, I was more firm. "Front page! Change it! Noon! Please!"

At that point, my team reluctantly concluded that, in fact,

changing the front page of the site on schedule was indeed part of the job, and it would get done—finally.

I couldn't figure out why I now had to ask three times when previously I only needed to say it once.

THE MAYOR OF CHICAGO LOSES IT

Perhaps the most extreme example of this frustrating phenomenon involved Lori Lightfoot, the mayor of Chicago. Chicago is a city of 2.7m people. It has 35,000 employees. Running Chicago is more like being the president of a small country than a municipal mayor. A huge chunk of the job involves meeting people—residents, lobbyists, political allies or opponents—and attending the endless committee meetings that keep a large city running. The mayor's schedule is heavily pressured.

Lightfoot had repeatedly asked her administrative staff to make sure she had personal office time scheduled every day so she could be alone to think, write, and make long-term plans for the city.

Unfortunately, her staff frequently caved to pressure from people who wanted to meet with the mayor, and (in her opinion) they failed to schedule her daily office time.

Out of patience, Lightfoot lost it. She went ballistic.

She sent a now-infamous email in which she wrote: "I need office time everyday! I need office time everyday! I need office time everyday! I need office time everyday! I need office time everyday! I need office time everyday! I need office time everyday! I need office time everyday! I need office time everyday! I need office time everyday! I need office time everyday! I need office time everyday! I need office time everyday! I need office time everyday! I need office time everyday! I need office time everyday!"

That's the same sentence, 16 times in a row.

"Not just once a week or some days, everyday!" she wrote, a further ten times after that.

And then, she wrote five times, "If this doesn't change immediately, I will just start unilaterally canceling things every day."

"Have I made myself clear, finally?!" (She wrote that sentence 13 times in the email.)

To be quite clear: This is not what good management looks like. A copy of the January 2021 email was eventually obtained by *The Chicago Tribune.* The paper wrote a story comparing Lightfoot to Jack Nicholson in the 1980 horror movie *The Shining*, in which Nicholson loses his mind and begins typing the words "All work and no play makes Jack a dull boy" thousands of times across hundreds of sheets of paper.

Nonetheless, once you start supervising a team of more than five people, you will begin to sympathize a little with Lightfoot.

"IN MOST ASPECTS OF LIFE, YOU NEED TO SAY SOMETHING ABOUT TWENTY TIMES BEFORE IT TRULY STARTS TO SINK IN"

I first heard the phrase "Repetition doesn't spoil the prayer" at a seminar in London given by former Google CEO Eric Schmidt and Jonathan Rosenberg, Google's former senior vice president of products. Schmidt was arguing that a big part of management is simply saying the same thing over and over again.

Google, of course, has tens of thousands of employees. Many more, even, than the City of Chicago. It turns out that Schmidt had the same problem that Lightfoot and I did, but on a much larger scale: "In most aspects of life, you need to say something about twenty times before it truly starts to sink in," Schmidt and Rosenberg say in their book, *How Google Works.*

"Say it a few times, people are too busy to even notice. A few more times, they start to become aware of a vague buzzing in their ears. By the time you've repeated it fifteen to twenty times you may be completely sick of it, but that's about the time that people are starting to get it."

Twenty times!

THE *CONE OF LEARNING*—AND WHY IT IS BULLSHIT

This idea—that repetition is a big part of management—isn't a new insight.

Most famously, in 1969 the academic researcher Edgar Dale suggested in his Cone of Learning model that people only retain about 20% of the information they are told verbally. The Cone of Learning is a diagram that looks like a pyramid divided into horizontal slices. The top of the pyramid shows that people only remember 10% of what they read. Underneath that, the progressively wider slices show they retain 20% of what they hear and, on the bottom-most slice, 90% of what they do. Dale's Cone of Learning suggests that having students do practical tasks in lessons is a more effective teaching method than just telling them the information.

EDGAR DALE'S CONE OF LEARNING

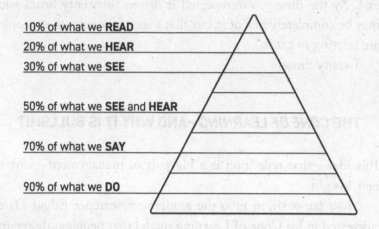

10% of what we **READ**

20% of what we **HEAR**

30% of what we **SEE**

50% of what we **SEE** and **HEAR**

70% of what we **SAY**

90% of what we **DO**

Dale's Cone has had a lot of influence on the teaching profession. At universities, it is common to tell students that they will likely only retain a small portion of the lectures they listen to. Thus taking careful notes and completing the homework assignments are the best ways to learn.

In management, the big takeaway from the Cone of Learning is that if people only remember 20% of what you are saying, then you need to say it to them about five times in order to create a 100% chance that any given staffer has taken on board what you just said.

Plot twist!

Dale's Cone of Learning has since been comprehensively debunked. It turns out there was no research to generate the 20% statistic! Dale's percentages were just made up.

But it certainly *feels* true when you become the manager of a team larger than three people. You will find yourself issuing the same instructions over and over again. It's a bit weird at first. "Why aren't they listening to me? Why are people ignoring what I tell them?"

Get used to it. It's not you. Your team isn't selectively forgetful.

It is simply that communication gets more complicated the more people you supervise. You will need to repeat yourself.

THE RULE OF FIVE KICKS IN

With just two other people, you can chat at your desks and everyone is on the same page.

Once you get to five people, communication becomes harder: the rule of five kicks in. Some people will sit further away and not be able to hear you. Someone will be out to lunch. Someone will be in the bathroom. Someone will be at a meeting with a client or a source. All of a sudden, communicating the same thing, at the same time, to more than five people is no longer simply about having a brief conversation.

The problem magnifies as your team gets larger. If you have a team larger than six people, you will probably also need a deputy underneath you to assist in managing them. Now you are delegating your communication to lieutenants and trusting them to communicate identical instructions to the people they supervise.

Like the childhood game of telephone, stuff gets lost in translation.

What you say is not what they hear: Let's say you are discussing with your team two possible options, A and B. You, as the manager, must make a decision to go with one of them. If you say, "I like A," it is likely that half your team will hear, "He hates B!" You may not hate B. The B choice may be totally fine, but B just isn't the right fit on this occasion. And yet, for some of your staff, you are now a B-hater.

So you need to repeat it.

You don't hate B. This is only really about A. It can take a long time—and much repetition—for everyone to realize that.

There is also inertia and fog in larger teams and companies.

People are receiving emails and instructions from multiple departments, all day long. For efficiency's sake, workers tend to ignore a large chunk of the messages directed at them. It is simply not possible to respond to your boss, the HR department, the legal folks, the office manager, clients, friends, and colleagues— and also get all your work done on time.

So workers take unconscious shortcuts. If they hear their boss issuing new instructions, they weigh those instructions against all the competing demands on their time, and also the possibility that one of their colleagues might complete the task so that they won't have to. Whenever there is collective responsibility, there is a tendency to hope someone else will do it—and that's how things *don't* get done.

You're going to feel like a broken record, going on about the new plan for the umpteenth time. Just remember that *the only person who is hearing this repeatedly is you*. Most employees were not in most meetings, did not receive most emails, and have not seen most of the presentations you will have sat through. For them, it is new. For every new employee, it is new.

YELLING AT PEOPLE ALL DAY IS NO LONGER ACCEPTABLE

The more people you have, the more diverse communication styles you will encounter among them.

Sadly, I am old enough to remember what working was like in the mid-1990s. At my first newspaper job there was no email and no voicemail. If you wanted to communicate with a colleague, you had to talk to them, face to face. For speed, it was perfectly acceptable to just stand up at your desk and yell across the room. In the newspaper business, speed is of the essence. Yelling at your colleagues was the quickest, surest way of getting stuff done. Everyone accepted that. It was normal. We weren't yelling in anger (mostly). We were yelling because it was easier. "Hey Jennifer! The cops say there is a fire in downtown Paterson! Can we get a photographer out there now please!" That kind of thing.

Today, however, employees no longer believe that being yelled at all day is acceptable.

How unreasonable!

Some prefer to read instructions in an email, so they can refer to it later for the details. Some individuals prefer to receive instructions verbally, in a face-to-face meeting. Some people prefer to receive messages in Slack, or whatever workplace chatroom software your company uses. Some workers have grown up in a headphones-only environment, and know nothing else. Getting through the headphones-at-work barrier can be a major communications challenge.

So, if you are running a team larger than six people, my advice is to communicate the same message through all the channels your company uses, one after the other:

- Same message in meetings.
- Same message in emails.
- Same message written on a whiteboard in the conference room.
- Same message in a paper memo handout.
- Same message in Slack, or whatever internal company messaging system you use.

That way, you reach everybody via their preferred medium, and everybody gets the same message. (Even if they are wearing headphones.)

It will feel like Groundhog Day, because you will be saying the same thing over and over again. Get used to it. Be patient. The oil tanker won't turn on a dime.

It turns out that a huge part of your job as a manager—most of it, in fact—is basically communication. People want to know what is going on. They want to know what the big picture is. What the company's plan is. What *your* plan is. They want to know what the company's standards are. What your expectations of them are. They want to know where they fit in. They want to know what you think good work looks like, and what poor performance looks like.

THE WAR AGAINST MUSHROOM FARMING

Terrible companies sometimes use a management tactic called mushroom farming. That's the school of thought that says you should keep people in the dark and feed them shit.

Mushroom farming is a terrible management strategy. Do not do this.

To combat mushroom farming, encourage your staff to ask questions about how and why things get done. You'll be surprised what they guess at—and their guesses often assume the worst.

I once had a member of staff who was convinced I was leaking information about his work to a PR person who was pressuring him heavily not to publish an investigation he was doing into a company that was about to go bankrupt.

This investigation was going to be deeply damaging to the company when we published it. The founders of the company were desperately trying to save their firm by negotiating new funding from their existing investors. Crucially, those investors did not know just how badly the company was being run. They had already sunk £14m (about $19m) into the company and were unlikely to get it back. Our report was going to lay the company bare, and thus possibly frighten away further investment. To make things even more complicated, one of the investors was a famous, eccentric, and litigious British billionaire property tycoon.

What the reporter did not realize was that after every phone conversation he had with the company's PR person, that PR person then immediately called me, because I was his boss. In her conversations with both of us, she cast doubts about what the other one was saying. She was trying to make his life difficult by dripping poison into our ears. (PR people really do behave like this!)

The PR strategy was successful: This writer became worried his work was being undermined by me and that I might kill his scoop. He confronted me about it, angry at the apparent betrayal.

In fact, the opposite was true. I wanted the story out as soon as possible because I thought it was a great exclusive. He had no idea that the PR person was playing us both against each other. As soon as he knew the full story, the black cloud dissipated. A single conversation ended weeks of low-level paranoia. It's amazing how much easier work becomes after a little bit of openness and transparency.

And yes, we published the story.

TEN-SECOND CHEAT SHEET

- Communicate all the time. Often, loudly, and in plain English. People want simple, clear instructions. They want to know what's going on, what the company news is, and so on. Tell them the goals, for both quality and quantity.

- Use all the channels to communicate all the messages. Different people attach different levels of importance to different communication media. Use them all: Email, face to face, direct messages, and your company's internal chat channels and bulletin boards.

- Be patient. The tanker won't turn on a dime.

- ⏱ Listen to staff, often. I meet with everyone I supervise directly at least once a week. Sometimes it's a brief 15-minute check-in. Other times it's an hour-long dissection of something really serious. I am talking to members of my team constantly throughout the day, as we go about our work, of course. And there are a million emails and Slack conversations. But these dedicated meetings are face-to-face time to make sure, in Dave's immortal words, that everyone knows "what the fuck is going on."

- ⏱ Repetition doesn't spoil the prayer. You will need to communicate everything at least three times—and maybe as many as 20—to staff before they finally take it on board and start doing it. Some days really will feel like Groundhog Day.

- ⏱ Repetition is necessary because what you say is not what people hear.

- ⏱ Keep no secrets. Try to be as transparent as possible.

- ⏱ Say "thank you" for everything. Literally, thank people all the time for the work they do, and the time they put in. Tell them you appreciate it. Say it out loud. You can defuse a large amount of job stress among your staff by saying, "Thank you for doing that, I really appreciate it. It was a lot of work and it did not go unnoticed. Great job."

II
PRODUCTIVITY

5

Prioritize & delete: The Eisenhower Matrix for increasing productivity

YOU are probably keen to get the best from your staff; to encourage them to work hard, to get better; and to see your team succeed. You want them to continuously become more productive.

The problem with asking everyone to work harder and get better is that it's a grim, relentless message to send to your people. No one wants to feel like they're on a hamster wheel. It is a recipe for burnout.

Employees generally work hard. It's actually rare, in my experience, to encounter a habitual office skiver trying to skate by, doing the least amount of work possible. Luckily, making your team more productive and reducing burnout turn out to be the exact same thing.

The following is a strategy to get both.

THE INTERNET IS TO BLAME FOR BURNOUT

First, let's discuss why the world of work currently seems so exhausting.

In the era before the internet replaced real life, your work stayed at work. Even in the early days of email, your email stayed at work. Your computer stayed at work, too. No one had a home computer. Your boss could maybe call you at home (on a landline!). But if you were out of the house when the boss called, you were unreachable.

It was normal to go home at night and not even think about work until the next morning. Weekends were completely free of work. There was no checking your messages on your phone. There was no opening the laptop late at night just to make sure. Even emergencies were dealt with the next day.

There was a hard border between work and private life.

Those days are gone.

Today, it's likely that your work email will be on your phone, and that your personal laptop is used as much for work as for leisure. Many bosses like to send messages at night. They may not be expecting their staff to act on them immediately—they are just trying to get a jump on the day ahead. But a lot of workers also like to check their messages at night. Not because they are eager to work into the small hours—they, like their bosses, are just trying to get a jump on the day ahead.

The result is that we're stuck in an always-on cycle of work. No one has any work-free mental space. Your office is now right there in your house, on your kitchen table, in your pocket. Burnout is a direct result of the internet and smartphones.

I am a victim of it too. While writing this chapter, I could think of only two times during the previous week when I had not reflexively checked my phone for work:

- When I was swimming at my local pool.

- When I was asleep.

It is not surprising that burnout is a problem if the only way to escape work is to become unconscious or hide underwater.

Your team is probably feeling it worse than you because bosses tend to underestimate the time their tasks take to complete. Here are some tactics I use to reduce burnout and increase productivity.

PRIORITIZE & DELETE: THE DIFFERENCE BETWEEN URGENT AND IMPORTANT

There is a famous quote that is often attributed to President Dwight D. Eisenhower: "What is important is seldom urgent and what is urgent is seldom important." In fact, historians and researchers who have tried to figure out whether he was the originator of this phrase now believe Eisenhower probably got it from someone else, and then repeated it in a speech at Northwestern University in Evanston, Illinois, in 1954.

In that speech Eisenhower said, "I have two kinds of problems, the urgent and the important. The urgent are not important, and the important are never urgent." Eisenhower said he heard the formulation from "a former college president," but didn't say who that was.

Since then, the phrase has taken on a life of its own because of Eisenhower's reputation for being able to get things done. He was a five-star general in World War II. He planned the invasion of Normandy in 1944, which won the war. He signed off on the creation of NASA, triggering the race to the moon. He sent federal troops to enforce the integration of schools in the segregationist Southern US. And he started the construction of the interstate highway system. For good measure, in his farewell speech in 1961, he invented the concept of "the military-industrial complex."

Clearly, Eisenhower was a productive dude.

Because of that, people have combed his life for clues to explain his prodigious ability to pull off huge accomplishments. They have even turned the phrase "what is important is seldom urgent and what is urgent is seldom important" into a system for making decisions. It's called the Eisenhower Matrix. In this system, you make a to-do list and rank the tasks in front of you based on whether they are "important" or "urgent," favoring importance over urgency.

The ranking works like this:

1. Urgent and important.
2. Important but not urgent.
3. Unimportant but urgent.
4. Unimportant and not urgent.

Obviously, you begin by tackling the No. 1 task. As you move down the list, you will quickly notice that your chances of completing all the tasks get worse and worse as time goes by. This is OK. No one cares if you don't complete the most trivial tasks on your list. The key is that you have tackled the most important things. (People really notice when you fail at important things!)

I am a big believer in to-do lists. To-do lists are a good way of demonstrating to yourself that there is no way you will be able to do everything on the list. And that, on its own, is a good way to set priorities for yourself and your teams. Get the top priorities done first, and don't worry if the less-important tasks fall by the wayside.

MAKE EVERYONE ELSE PRIORITIZE TOO

Importantly, you have to make everyone else on your team do this too.

Sometimes I ask colleagues to complete an important new task, and the response I get is, "I'm too busy with all this other work!" We have all groaned inwardly when our bosses have asked us to do some new thing. "Can't they see I am already busy?!"

Whenever I encounter an employee who claims they are too busy, I ask them to tell me everything they are working on. I write it down in a list. Sure enough, they have a lot on their plate. Then I say, "OK, let's prioritize this work. Let's have you doing the most important stuff first. And if you don't get to the least important stuff—fine. No one will care."

DELETE THE THREE LEAST IMPORTANT TASKS FROM EVERYONE'S TO-DO LIST

The charm of the prioritize & delete method is that the bottom-most tasks on each day's list are self-deleting. If you can't get to them, they don't happen.

In real life, however, many employees do not feel they have the power or permission to drop tasks while they are at work. So you need to make it absolutely clear to members of your team that you will happily rank their priorities for them and delete their more trivial tasks. To emphasize the advantage of prioritizing, I say: "If you feel there is too much on your plate, let me delete the three least important tasks on your list."

This gets people's attention. By saying you'll *take away* work from an employee, you are actually presenting the new set of priorities as an advantage for them—less work!

You have to be serious about this. You cannot fix burnout

by giving people extra work. But you can go a long way to ameliorating it by prioritizing the work people are doing—and by canceling the most trivial tasks that are bogging down your team.

In practice, I usually find that my offer of taking work away is politely rebuffed. Folks often prefer to retain control of their own to-do lists. They want to decide for themselves what gets dropped, not you. They want to be in control of their own work. That's a good outcome, as long as you both agree on the priority tasks at the top of the list that will definitely get done, and can accept that the ones on the bottom will not.

GIVE YOUR STAFF THE RIGHT TO PRIORITIZE— AND TO FORCE YOU TO DO IT TOO

Staff tend not to want to say that they are overworked. They feel it makes them look incompetent. So they keep saying *yes* to their bosses until something collapses. However, the default setting of management is that you're constantly asking staff to do new things, start new projects, or solve new problems. You're generally adding tasks rather than taking them away. So if you want your staff to concentrate on the top priority tasks, then you have to grant people the right to tell you, "This is too much—can you prioritize what you want?" That will force *you* to rationalize your priorities for *them*.

Prioritizing is a two-way street. You need to require it of *them*, but they also need to be able to get it from *you*.

MAKE YOUR TOP PERFORMERS DO LESS

There's a cynical saying in management circles that I hear a lot: "If you want something done, give it to a busy person!"

This quote originates from 1856, when it was said by the Rev. W.J. Kennedy, a British inspector of schools for Lancashire and the Isle of Man. The original quote from one of his reports was: "If you want any business done for you, you should ask a busy man to do it."

This is terrible advice for managers.

If you were the manager of Formula 1 champion Lewis Hamilton, you wouldn't ask him to do the laundry for the rest of his teammates before every race, would you? Of course not. That would be ridiculous. You want Lewis Hamilton to concentrate on one thing: driving fast. He should not be worrying about the crew's uniforms.

So one of your priorities should be to declutter the agendas of your most productive people. Your rock stars are the ones who will get your team where it needs to go. The overperformers are going to set the pace. The less experienced staff will learn from them and their success.

Because your top performers are so good at their jobs, it will be tempting to pile more work onto them.

Wrong.

Clear the way for them. Let them focus on the most important work, and nothing else.

You should do the same thing as a manager: Focus on your top performers. This is a notion that you'll hear managers talking a lot about, calling it the 80–20 rule. It's not really a rule. It's more of an aphorism. For managers it suggests that you get 80% of your results from 20% of your staff. Don't worry about whether 80–20 is literally true or not. That's not the point. What is important is that it will certainly *feel* as if the top 20% of your people are delivering the majority of your results.

That means you should try to invest a much larger portion of your time on the 20% of your people who are your top performers. This will get you your best results. The corollary of the rule is that you, as the manager, do not want to spend the majority of your time on your worst performers—that is a poor way to leverage your time.

You will notice that prioritizing, focusing on the most important work, ignoring trivial tasks, and actively making people do less are extensions of a theme we discussed earlier in the book: figuring out what works, and figuring out what does not. That's deliberate. Your job as a manager is to constantly reiterate this process: Lean into the stuff that works, and drop the stuff that doesn't move the needle.

TEN-SECOND CHEAT SHEET

- ⌚ Make your entire team prioritize their work. Have them tackle the most important things first.

- ⌚ It's OK if the less important things don't get done. No one cares.

- ⌚ Be serious about prioritizing the important, must-do tasks, and be equally serious about not caring about the trivial stuff that is low down on the list.

- ⌚ Doing less is the same thing as prioritizing.

- ⌚ People burn out because they are trying to do everything. It is much more important that they do only the most important things.

- ⌚ Delete the three least-important tasks from everyone's to-do list.

⌚ Give your staff the right to force you to prioritize their work.

⌚ Remember the 80–20 rule: You will probably get 80% of your results from the top 20% of your people. Use that as a guide for where to invest your time.

⌚ Limit email to certain hours of the day. Try not to send messages to your staff before the official start or after the official end of the work day.

⌚ When you are trying to set priorities for yourself or anyone else, handwritten to-do lists really work.

6

Whales & fails:
How to get good work
out of your team

EARLIER in this book I suggested that on your first day as a new manager, you should ask all staff what they think is working well, and what is not, so that you can draw up a plan that invests more of your team's time and resources into the successful stuff, and consciously walk away from activities that are a waste of time. Don't fool yourself into thinking that you will only need to make one plan, once. Make it your constant everyday mission, an ongoing process.

I have a name for this process: whales & fails. I recommend you schedule a regular meeting with your team in which colleagues describe their whales & fails. A whale is a big success. A fail is—you guessed it—a failure.

CELEBRATE AND EXPLAIN THE WHALES

Crucially, in such a meeting, each person should explain aloud why the whale they worked on was successful. It is not enough to say, "We worked on this project, and it was successful." You want to know exactly why that product or service was a hit, and to be able to show that with numbers. Success isn't based on magic or faith. You need specifics.

Did the product offer something different that no other company has? Was the service cheaper than the competition? Did you make it easier for customers to deal with your company than your rivals? Did you have superior social media tactics? Was your marketing or PR strategy faster or more witty?

Superior work doesn't happen simply because a manager thinks it is a good idea. Companies have to earn their customers and users.

There are myriad reasons why one offering might become a huge hit while the next one sinks without trace. Your staff need to be able to explain what happened and why.

Not only does this teach you what your customers like, but the process of explaining it generates new ideas and themes for related work that might be equally successful. The generation of new ideas on its own has an important value (and we'll discuss this later in the book).

It is also an opportunity for you and your colleagues to applaud great new work. "Praise it when you see it" is a good mantra to use here. (It actually originates from a method of encouraging good behavior in small children—but let's gloss over that!) An important part of management is reinforcing good performance at work. If someone gets something right, let them know. If someone goes above and beyond the call of duty, let them know. Praise good work often. Every time you see it. Frequent recognition and thanks go a long way. (Say "thank you" for everything!)

You should also praise good work *in public*. Consider a teamwide email or a kudos note to your CEO with your colleagues cc'd when someone on your team excels. Telling people they did good work isn't just about recognizing that an individual is doing well. It is also about setting the tone for other people on your team. If they see you telling Rebecca that you really liked that last project she completed, then the secondary message you will be communicating to all staff is, "This is what good work looks like—be like Rebecca." Praise it when you see it is not just about praise but about demonstrating a model to everyone else.

Most importantly for you as a manager, regularly reviewing the successes of everyone on your team will show you patterns emerging and changing over time. Your job as a leader is to make your people more productive, more successful. So being able to clearly identify exactly how success happens—and to be able to repeat it with other members of your staff—is crucial.

Praise the less obvious stuff, too. When I am working late, and the office cleaners come round and empty everyone's trash cans, I like to see how many people say "thank you" when their crumpled paper and old sandwich wrappers are taken away. It's never 100%. Some people seem almost embarrassed to talk to cleaners. And yet most offices would turn into landfill sites within days if the janitors didn't show up. An army needs soldiers as well as generals, otherwise it is going nowhere. So don't forget to say "thank you" to the soldiers too.

ACTIVELY STOP THE FAILS—AND UNDERSTAND WHY

Crucially, in a whales & fails meeting each colleague should also describe a failure. When a product doesn't resonate with your customers, it is not usually down to mere bad luck. Often, in hindsight, you can see why a flop was a flop.

The price was too high. Your marketing was filled with technical jargon. The instructions were confusing or unhelpful. The packet design was boring. Maybe the idea sounded great when you planned it in the conference room, but out in the real world few people actually needed it or thought it was interesting.

Again, the act of articulating why something failed helps you to consciously avoid such mistakes in the future.

Everyone wants to learn from success but, interestingly, it is failure that teaches us the most. Learning quickly that something isn't working, and dropping it, will make your team much more productive, more quickly, than any other single tactic.

That's why articulating aloud both the successes and the failures is so important.

WHALES & FAILS IMPROVES TOTAL PERFORMANCE OVER TIME WITHOUT THE NEED FOR NEW STAFF OR NEW SKILLS

There is another reason that whales & fails works so well: mathematics.

Consider how averages work. You probably learned how to calculate an average in high-school math class. It's easy—you add up all your data points, and then divide the total by the number of people that generated them. That gives you an average performance for all the people in the group.

The average will contain the worst score and the best score. Now let's assume that your workers are all of roughly equal ability but the products they are working on vary in how popular they are with your customers. Obviously, if you can stop the person with the worst score from repeating that score by moving them to an area of your business that produces better results you will mechanically move the average performance of your entire team upward.

Here's a theoretical example that is so simple it's insulting. But I am going to walk you through it anyway because I want you to understand how averages work at a visceral, gut level, and how to use them to your advantage.

Let's say you work at a car dealership, which sells only red, yellow, and green cars. You have three salespeople: Tom, Dick, and Harriet. Tom is responsible for selling yellow cars, Dick sells green cars, and Harriet sells red cars. Let's also assume that all three salespeople are equally capable as sellers—there are no duds on this team. The only difference between them is their responsibility for selling a specific color of car.

In their first month on the job, their sales record looks like this:

CAR DEALERSHIP SALES, FIRST MONTH

 = 10 cars

Tom: 10 yellow cars sold

Dick: 5 green cars sold

Harriet: 3 red cars sold

Total: 18 cars sold (6 cars each on average)

What is going on here?

Clearly, customers don't seem to like the red cars much. They aren't terribly keen on the green cars either. But the yellow cars are a big hit.

The yellow cars are your whales. The red cars are the fails. So you decide to apply the whales & fails process, incrementally. By simply directing Harriet to sell yellow cars, she might also sell ten cars per month. If that happened in the following month, the results would look like this:

CAR DEALERSHIP SALES, SECOND MONTH: AFTER MOVING ONE EMPLOYEE FROM THE WORST- TO THE BEST-SELLING CAR

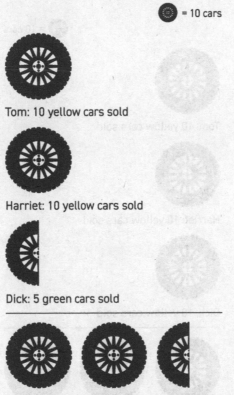

= 10 cars

Tom: 10 yellow cars sold

Harriet: 10 yellow cars sold

Dick: 5 green cars sold

Total: 25 cars sold (8.3 cars each on average)

Now, both Tom and Harriet are working on projects that are whales. By comparison, the green cars that are Dick's responsibility currently look like fails.

Obviously, if you then also moved Dick onto the yellow salesforce, the average would improve even more—it would be ten cars per month for each of the three sellers. Your total sales would go up to 30 cars a month, when previously it was 18 cars per month. That's a 67% increase in sales from where you started:

CAR DEALERSHIP SALES, THIRD MONTH: AFTER MOVING ALL EMPLOYEES TO THE BEST-SELLING CAR

= 10 cars

Tom: 10 yellow cars sold

Harriet: 10 yellow cars sold

Dick: 10 yellow cars sold

Total: 30 cars sold (10 cars each on average)

Importantly, the *average* and the *total* went up without you having to hire any extra staff. You simply changed what the staff were doing. You stopped Harriet and Dick from working on the unsuccessful cars (the fails) and moved them to the high-performing cars (the whales).

Now consider what you did *not* do: You didn't force Harriet or Dick to work harder or faster. None of your staff improved their performance. They didn't need to develop new skills or acquire new expertise. They didn't come in early or work late. No one had to work on the weekend. But you got the results anyway, simply by moving them off low-value tasks and moving them onto high-performing tasks.

This is the value of whales & fails. It's not merely about making individuals more productive or celebrating success—although both of those things are great. It's about the benefit of mechanically moving up both the average performance of your team and the total results they get, *without requiring any extra work, skill, or staff.*

As a manager, if you are continually dropping the least successful tasks and moving people over to the more successful tasks, and if you are using a whales & fails process to generate new ideas that might be even better than your current top performers, you are likely to see continual incremental gains.

Most importantly, you do not need to be a superhuman management genius to do this. You just need to figure out what an average performance on your team looks like, and then take action to move the average up a bit.

TEN-SECOND CHEAT SHEET

- Use the whales & fails method: Insist that staff tell you what worked and explain why it worked, then tell you what failed and why it failed.

- Figure out what gets above-average results—and then do more of it.

- Praise success when you see it, so that everyone gets the message.

- Use examples of success to generate new ideas about other types of work, products or services that might also be successful.

- Stop work on underperforming tasks.

- Move staff from underperforming areas to projects that overperform the average.

- Moving staff away from fails toward the whales improves total performance over time.

- The whales & fails process will generate increased performance over time without the need to add new staff, and without the need for your staff to work harder.

7

The incredible power of being slightly better than average

SIR ALEX FERGUSON, the former manager of Manchester United, was arguably the greatest sports manager of all time. His team won the English Premier League 13 times, the FA Cup five times, and the UEFA Champions League twice. Ferguson was so successful, for so long, that he won trophies most people have forgotten existed. In some cases they literally no longer exist. Does anyone remember the Intercontinental Cup, which Manchester United won in 1999? Me neither. The tournament is no longer alive.

Regardless, the point is that he was very successful indeed as a soccer manager. Unusually successful. In 2021, Ferguson published a book of management advice titled *Leading*. The implicit promise of *Leading* is that if you can learn from Ferguson's insights, then maybe you too can become the greatest manager of all time.

Fat chance.

This is not going to happen.

In reality, a lot of space is wasted in the business press in the hope of inspiring you to become a superstar business leader. Business advice books tend to focus on people like Apple founder Steve Jobs,

General Electric boss Jack Welch, Facebook and Palantir investor Peter Thiel, stock market maven Warren Buffett, and so on.

No doubt, these people have had amazing careers. But they are also statistical anomalies. They are wild outliers. They are the data points at the far end of the bell curve. Their performance is not common. While it would be nice if it was possible to become as good at management as Alex Ferguson simply by reading his book, that is extremely unlikely. The vast majority of managers—in football or business—are nowhere near that successful.

So let's be realistic.

YOU ARE NOT GOING TO BE THE GREATEST MANAGER OF ALL TIME

Don't worry, because being the greatest ever is not actually necessary.

To become an over-performing manager—someone who succeeds because their teams do better than others—you need to focus on something much easier: the incredible power of being slightly better than average.

"Slightly better than average!" does not sound like the most inspiring rallying cry, admittedly.

But bear with me.

In the last chapter I focused on why it is important to track the performance of your team, figure out what an average performance looks like, and then move people from underperforming tasks to overperforming tasks. That tactic alone gets improved performance from an entire team without anyone needing to improve as an individual or even do any extra work. Being able to calculate an average and then act on it is an important managerial skill.

Now I want to introduce a second concept from math that is equally important: compounding.

HOW TO GET COMPOUNDING GROWTH SUCCESS

Compounding is a mathematical term that usually describes how your money grows when banks pay interest on it. If you have $100 in a savings account, and you get 5% in simple interest, you will have $105 by the end of the year:

$$\$100 + 5\% = \$105$$

The next year you will have $110.25, because the 5% additional interest in the second year compounded on top of the interest you received in the first year:

$$\$100 + 5\% = \$105$$

and then...

$$\$105 + 5\% = \$110.25.$$

Notably, at the end of the second year, your savings are more than 10% greater than they were at the beginning even though your interest rate is half that—just 5%.

Compounding has *doubled* your gains even though the rate at which your gains took place stayed the *same*. Continuous gains, compounded on top of each other, will grow your total performance—forever.

THE VALUE OF *JUST A LITTLE BIT MORE*

Let's go back to our fictional car dealership with three salespeople. By the third month, we moved everyone into yellow car sales and everyone sold ten cars per month, for a total of 30 cars. Here's that table again:

CAR DEALERSHIP SALES, THIRD MONTH: AFTER MOVING ALL EMPLOYEES TO THE BEST-SELLING CAR

 = 10 cars

Tom: 10 yellow cars sold

Harriet: 10 yellow cars sold

Dick: 10 yellow cars sold

Total: 30 cars sold (10 cars each on average)

We achieved this without any improvement in individual performance (remember, they were all equally good at sales).

Now let's say you ask the team to collectively sell just *one* more car next month. This doesn't sound unreasonable. It isn't a big leap to go from 30 cars to 31 cars.

And let's also say you ask them to sell one more car than the previous month, *every month*.

After just one year you will have sold 428 cars in total. Had you changed nothing you would have sold only 234 cars. That's an 83% increase in sales simply because:

- You applied the whales & fails analysis, and moved all the salespeople to the most successful product.
- And then you asked them to compound their gains by being just a little bit more successful each month.

Remember, we started this hypothetical example with a team that sold only 18 cars per month, back in the days when two-thirds of your team were wasting their time on the unpopular red and green cars.

The mathematics are not difficult, but I want to burn this into your brain, so here are the two sets of results side by side:

CAR DEALERSHIP MONTHLY SALES AFTER MOVING ALL EMPLOYEES TO THE BEST-SELLING CAR AND WITH INCREMENTAL IMPROVEMENT

 = 10 cars

Month 1: 18 cars ... no change

Month 2: 25 cars ... after moving Harriet to the yellow cars

Month 3: 30 cars ... after moving all staff to the yellow cars

Month 4: 31 cars ... after asking all staff to sell one more car than they sold in the previous month

Month 5: 32 cars ... after asking all staff to sell one more car than they sold in the previous month

Month 6: 33 cars ... after asking all staff to sell one more car than they sold in the previous month

Month 7: 34 cars ... after asking all staff to sell one more car than they sold in the previous month

Month 8: 35 cars ... after asking all staff to sell one more car than they sold in the previous month

Month 9: 36 cars ... after asking all staff to sell one more car than they sold in the previous month

Month 10: 37 cars ... after asking all staff to sell one more car than they sold in the previous month

Month 11: 38 cars ... after asking all staff to sell one more car than they sold in the previous month

Month 12: 39 cars ... after asking all staff to sell one more car than they sold in the previous month

Month 13: 40 cars ... after asking all staff to sell one more car than they sold in the previous month

Total: 428 cars sold

Although the team is now selling ten more yellow cars per month than a year ago (40 cars, up from 30 cars), divided between the three of them, each salesperson only needs to sell three or four more cars per month to get there—again, not a mammoth challenge.

Here's what would have happened if you had done nothing:

CAR DEALERSHIP MONTHLY SALES IF YOU HAD MADE NO STAFFING CHANGES AND WITH ZERO INCREMENTAL IMPROVEMENT:

◉ = 10 cars

◉ ◉ Month 1: 18 cars

◉ ◉ Month 2: 18 cars

◉ ◉ Month 3: 18 cars

◉ ◉ Month 4: 18 cars

◉ ◉ Month 5: 18 cars

◉ ◉ Month 6: 18 cars

◉ ◉ Month 7: 18 cars

◉ ◉ Month 8: 18 cars

◉ ◉ Month 9: 18 cars

◉ ◉ Month 10: 18 cars

◉ ◉ Month 11: 18 cars

◉ ◉ Month 12: 18 cars

◉ ◉ Month 13: 18 cars

Total: 234 cars sold

Even if you *only* applied the whales & fails process and then did nothing more—i.e., did not ask the salespeople to increase their sales—you would have continued to sell 30 cars per month, for a total of 373 cars over the 13 months. That alone would have been a 59% increase in sales over the starting point—*even without requiring any extra work, skill, or staff.*

Total sales under all three conditions:

- Did nothing: 234 cars sold
- Used whales & fails: 373 cars sold
- Used whales & fails and asked for incremental improvement: 428 cars sold

SUCCESS IS A WAR OF ACCRETION

Suddenly, a slight improvement in average performance has become an Olympian feat. Sure, doing a little bit extra each month requires work. No denying it. But it won't feel like you're asking people to suddenly perform superhuman leaps. Every time you stop doing an underperforming task in favor of an overperforming task, you are incrementally moving your average performance upward, and hopefully building on that next month, too.

This is what you are aiming for over the long term: Figuring out the whales & fails, moving your resources to the most productive tasks, looking for incremental improvements, and compounding your gains.

This is how you get growth. Not by yelling at people. Not by punishing poor performers. Simply by getting slightly better as each month goes by.

Being consistently slightly better than average is going to make your long-term performance exceptional because constant, continuous, incremental improvements build on each other until you get where you need to go.

This is important. Figuring out how to get constant, continuous, incremental improvements is the most potent weapon you have as a manager. In the real world, results won't come as smoothly as this mathematical example. In the real world, it will be bumpy. A salesperson cannot sell one extra car every month *forever*. You will have to apply some judgment as the results come in. Part of that judgment may be hiring new salespeople to boost the team.

MANCHESTER UNITED'S ALEX FERGUSON KNOWS THIS BETTER THAN ANYONE, OF COURSE

When Ferguson got the job in 1986, he inherited players who drank too much and were not fit enough to play at the top level. Manchester United finished 11th, 11th, and 13th in three of his first four years at the helm—a dismal set of results. The team initially performed so poorly that there were calls for Ferguson to be sacked. During the 1989–1990 season a banner appeared at Old Trafford that said, "Three years of excuses and it's still crap... ta-ra [goodbye] Fergie."

It took Ferguson six years—making gradual improvements, selling some players and adding new ones—before United won their first league championship under him. Apparently, compounding smaller gains over time and slowly improving your team's average performance does indeed get you where you want to go.

TEN-SECOND CHEAT SHEET

- You don't have to be a superstar: You just have to be slightly better than average. Success is a war of accretion.

- Constant improvement: Figuring out how to get constant, continuous, incremental improvements, where the gains are repeatedly compounded, is the most potent weapon you have as a manager.

- Gain a little more each month: Set realistic, achievable goals for growing your team's results each month.

- Grow for the long term: Growth is growth. Over time, it will get you where you want to go.

- Compound your gains for outsize results: Small amounts of repeated extra effort produce greater gains over time.

8

How new ideas improve performance: The 2018 Nobel Prize in Economics

AT this point you might reasonably be asking, "This hypothetical car dealership is all very well, but how do I know this is going to work for me in real life?"

There are two reasons you can expect this to happen:

1. **People tend to become better at their jobs over time.** Your staff's experience and skills will build and improve as the months go by, and that will likely translate into better results.

2. **New ideas drive the heart of economic growth.** New ideas are not scarce. They don't run out. They are not part of a zero-sum game. They are free. There is an infinite supply of them.

The first reason is a truism, so I won't spend much time on it. Just remember what it was like on your first day in a new job. There was so much to learn. Everything seemed so difficult. Everything took so much time. By the end of your first day, you were mentally and physically exhausted from trying to remember so much new stuff.

But after a few months, the basics of your new job became so familiar that you executed them without thinking. You got faster. You made fewer mistakes. The quality of your work went up. Your performance improved. This is as true for pharmaceutical research as it is for waiting tables in a restaurant.

For managers, this is an amazing built-in advantage. As long as your people want to work, and are applying themselves diligently, they will get better at what they do over time.

NEW IDEAS GENERATE GROWTH

The second reason—that new ideas generate economic growth— is poorly understood. It is so poorly understood that it was only first described with any cogency in 1990. That was when economist Paul Romer of the University of Chicago—and later New York University—published a dense, technical academic paper that described a way to value ideas, and to measure how they contribute to economic growth.

Before Romer came along, most people understood economics as being about scarcity—in particular, the scarcity of goods or services. If I buy a ticket to see a concert, it means there are now fewer tickets left for everyone else to buy. The remaining number of tickets may be so small that distortions in the concert-ticket market may set in: People will become willing to sell their tickets to others at a profit. Ticket touts will appear outside the venue trying to buy spare tickets cheaply in order to sell them at a higher price before the show begins.

At the concert itself, more money will be generated by the venue selling drinks at the bar. Drinks will be restricted to the people who have money to buy them, and to those who are willing to miss parts of the show to stand in line to get them. The provision of drinks will be a function of the scarcity of your money, the limited speed at which the bartenders can serve the crowd, and the time the venue is required to stop serving alcohol at the end of the night.

By the time your favorite rock band has played its last encore, their simple decision to sell tickets for a concert will have generated a mini-economy: The rock band creates something of value (concert tickets), for which the supply is limited (scarcity), and then other customers and ticket touts arbitrage the value of those goods via new, secondary trading (the stock market works a bit like this.) At the same time, other vendors step in to sell drinks (complementary goods and services) which wouldn't exist if the band had not staged the concert.

Concert halls cannot stage an infinite number of concerts. And there is a limited number of bands that people will pay to see. These limits create the scarcity we are talking about. That scarcity imposes a value on the available tickets. Ultimately, the total amount of economic activity generated is far greater than the initial value of the tickets sold.

In economics, goods are limited—or scarce—as far as most people are concerned. And that scarcity creates value and growth.

Romer described scarce goods and services like this using the word *rivalrous*, because one concert ticket for me is one concert ticket that you cannot have.

IDEAS AND NEW TECHNOLOGY ARE INFINITELY PLENTIFUL

However, Romer believed that none of this describes the effect of ideas, at the level of either an individual company or an entire country.

That is because ideas are not scarce. Anyone can have a new idea. If I have an idea, it does not mean that you cannot also have the same idea. We can all have as many ideas as we like. Ideas are therefore *non-rivalrous*, to use Romer's terminology.

Ideas show up in the concrete form of new technology. You can buy a software package that makes it easier to analyze your company's sales results. Let's say this new software contains a sophisticated artificial intelligence program that can suggest new sales strategies you had not previously thought of. This might give you a tangible advantage over competing companies.

But the idea for the software—and the software itself—is not scarce. Your competitive rivals can buy the same software and get the same advantages. Software programs are not like concert tickets. Owning one does not prevent other people from possessing it too.

It's not just software. You can see non-rivalrous new ideas popping up all over the place. Yes, tickets to see your favorite band may be scarce. But that doesn't stop anyone else forming a new band and trying to make better music. Just because one drug company has created a vaccine, it does not prevent other companies from using the same principles of inoculation to create better versions of that vaccine or different vaccines for other diseases. Tesla's ability to sell an electric car that can travel 200 miles between charges does not prevent another company from making a better car that can go even further. New ideas emerge everywhere, most frequently in the form of new technologies.

An idea doesn't become more scarce just because one person has it. Ideas don't become depleted over time, like a reservoir of water or an oil well. Everyone can use the idea. All at once. Everywhere.

That creates a vast amount of new economic growth and value, Romer argued. The notion that good ideas create new economic growth sounds incredibly obvious, now that you have heard it. But measuring their value accurately, and proving it mathematically, is not simple. This was Romer's contribution. He demonstrated it to be true in a series of models using very difficult algebra, which you will be grateful I did not reproduce here.

It took another 18 years for the rest of the world to figure out that Romer had been right. In 2018 he was awarded the Nobel Prize in Economics.

HOW DOES ALL THIS APPLY TO YOU?

The economic value of new ideas—coupled with the ever-increasing expertise of your staff—means that, as a manager, you have the wind at your back. The environment around you is constantly improving. This month, your staff are slightly better at their work than they were last month, because they have one more month of experience. They are able to execute their work slightly faster, with slightly fewer errors, than before.

More experience brings more sophistication —and therefore more power and more value.

Their colleagues in other teams—HR, legal, tech support, marketing—are also getting slightly better as time goes by. Their assistance becomes quicker and more effective every day.

The technology around you is getting better all the time, too. The phone in your hand today is more sophisticated than the one you owned a year ago, or the year before that. The car you drive today is more economical than the car you owned five years ago. The computer you are using today is faster and more reliable than the one you had two years ago.

And the ideas that you and your staff are generating about how to improve your work are getting better and more powerful every day. Most importantly, a whales & fails analysis will constantly generate new ideas to improve their work (and help you to axe the tasks that aren't getting results).

Getting a continuous, slightly better than average performance from a team is a realistic, achievable goal, and you can compound those gains over time because your team's ongoing experience and new ideas are generating incremental improvements all around you, all the time.

You and your teams are floating in an ocean of constant improvement, and your boats are being borne forward by that.

TEN-SECOND CHEAT SHEET

- ⊘ People tend to become better at their jobs over time.

- ⊘ This will help you generate compounding gains in performance.

- ⊘ New ideas are free, and create tangible lasting value.

- ⊘ The whales & fails method will help you strategize around the best ideas.

- ⊘ The rising tide of improved experience and new ideas is working in your favor.

9

The strip-club problem and why good data is the solution

HISTORICALLY, the automobile industry has been a guys' business. Men worked in the car factories. More men managed those men in the corporate headquarters. There was also a satellite world of parts suppliers—largely staffed by men. And a further tranche of men worked in the dealerships that sold the cars.

The industry was so chauvinistic that by the 1980s and 1990s, a lot of crucial deals and meetings in the automobile industry took place in the topless bars of Detroit. By 1997 there were 75 (!) strip clubs within a short drive of the big three Detroit carmakers. To put that in perspective, there were more than double the number of strip clubs in the neighborhood of Ford, Chrysler, and General Motors at the time than currently exist in all of Las Vegas.

The car companies had created their own red light district. A typical annual expenses bill for a single automobile executive who regularly wined and dined clients in the clubs might run to $40,000, *The New York Times* reported. Executives would even eat lunch at strip clubs, spending hundreds of dollars per person. One venue, Jon-Jon's—a mile from a GM site in Warren, Michigan, with 20,000 staff—had so many car executives as customers that it installed a digital business news ticker in its bar to keep clients updated during the day.

The strip club situation in Detroit became so normal that it distorted hiring decisions at car companies. One executive who spoke to *The Times* said his sales staff were entertaining potential clients at strip clubs twice a week, and this meant he could not hire women. "If I have a certain amount of my client base that likes to come here, which is mostly male, would it be a smart business decision on my part to assign that account to a woman salesperson?" he said.

Eventually, female employees sued the car companies. One woman claimed her male colleagues' expense budgets were seven times greater than hers because they spent so much at adult entertainment venues while she was taking clients to the ice-skating rink.

Clearly, this was insane.

Vital business decisions in America's most important manufacturing industry were being mediated via lap dances. An entire class of workers—women—was excluded because they weren't comfortable, or weren't invited, to do business in sex-oriented establishments.

Detroit is an extreme example. But back before the internet, a lot of corporate management was done like this: It was about "relationships," and that often meant socializing and networking. Not usually in strip clubs, of course. But in restaurants and bars, and on golf courses.

I once worked for a magazine where, every Thursday night, the editor would place his corporate American Express card behind the bar of Ben Benson's steakhouse in Manhattan. The editorial staff would drink martinis into the small hours. How this helped us publish a magazine is anyone's guess. But everyone went. Everyone who wanted to get promoted, that is.

More typically, it is common—even today—for your boss to

simply form an opinion of you based on their personal interactions with you, or vague anecdotal memories, and assess your performance based on that. You might advance if your boss likes you, if you talk a good game, if you sit close to your boss in the office rather than in the farthest corner, or if your boss can relate to you. This is how old boys' networks become crucial to your career advancement.

The manifestly dumb aspect of it all is that work is not a popularity contest; it is a getting-things-done contest. Your career should not be dependent on a series of completely random social qualities that may be unrelated to your work. It also means those bosses make bad decisions, because their impressions of the people working for them came from schmoozing and not from actual data about the quality of their work.

Needless to say, historically this has militated heavily against anyone who has less time in their lives for martinis. Or golf. Or strippers.

As a manager, you have a chance to do a lot better. And the way to do that is through data.

DATA IS THE WAY

You want to treat people fairly and objectively. You also want to encourage the best performers at work, regardless of their social skills. The way to do that is by giving people very clear, measurable goals and by collecting objective performance data to demonstrate that.

The key is *measurable*.

Data should be tangible, checkable, and measurable. At many digital media companies, for instance, management looks at traffic on websites, apps downloaded, subscriptions sold, and sales of media products to advertisers. Your company will have equivalent metrics. They might be sales, customers seen, products made, or projects completed.

Be serious about this. At the beginning of every month, have your teams collect and present data to you on their performance against the goals you set.

And you should do the same upward, to your bosses. This sounds pettifogging, but it is actually liberating. It frees your staff from the tyranny of having their compensation decided by a boss who might not like them, or someone who simply comes from a different social circle.

The best kind of data is visual data. You want to avoid showing someone a spreadsheet that consists of a vast sea of raw numbers in columns and rows. Make the data visual—in the form of charts and graphs. It is the easiest way to spot patterns, growth, and weaknesses. The data should speak for itself.

I use Google Sheets because it is free and its files can be easily imported into other software programs. Microsoft Excel is also popular. If you have never used spreadsheets to make charts before, I would highly recommend taking a class, persuading a friend to teach you, or watching a series of YouTube video tutorials in order to master the basics.

Cranking out your own performance data makes you intimately familiar with how and why that data changes over time. Don't rely on others to track your team's performance for you.

Lastly, a month-over-month snapshot of data is generally useless. It might feel nice to know that your May numbers were better than your April numbers. That would suggest that you are doing well. But it is just a snapshot. If your data omits that your *current* May numbers are well below May of *last year*, then you're not seeing the real problem. So collect data trends over the long term, not just a month or two.

BE WARNED: DATA WILL ATTEMPT TO DROWN YOU

OK, so everyone you supervise is now generating good data and you are making sophisticated decisions because of it.

Hooray.

You are now likely to encounter the opposite problem—drowning in data. For every company that collects too little data and is guided by the gut instincts of its bosses, there are ten firms where staff are submerged under vast seas of information. A friend of mine once discovered that over time, she had been given 54 different spreadsheets or dashboards through which to analyze her company's results. Clearly, her data analysis team was excellent—and prolific! But there is no way she could use 54 different metrics to make meaningful decisions. In reality, she looked at a handful of them and ignored the rest.

You can use two methods from this book to figure out which data sources you should focus on and which you should ignore. Prioritize & delete will help you rank your data based on its importance to you. And whales & fails, similarly, will help you ignore data sources that produce more noise than signal.

TEN-SECOND CHEAT SHEET

⌚ If a significant portion of your business is being conducted through strip clubs, you are probably going wrong!

⌚ Do not conduct "management by anecdote." Do not judge your staff by way of personal impressions, or feelings, or relationships.

⌚ Avoid making decisions based on subjective factors, such as whether an employee "talks a good game." Work is not a popularity contest. It is a getting-things-done contest.

⌚ Even trivial things—such as whether a staffer sits close to your desk or far away—can mislead you into making bad decisions.

⌚ Treat people fairly and objectively by giving them clear, measurable goals, and by collecting objective performance data.

⌚ The data should be tangible, measurable, and checkable.

⌚ Have your teams collect and present their performance data against the goals you set.

⌚ The best kind of data is visual data. Data in the form of charts and graphs is the easiest way to spot trends and weaknesses.

⌚ Look for long-term patterns in the data, not just month-to-month improvement.

10

The cure for acne and the difference between good data and good judgment

THE next problem to watch out for is the habit of allowing the spreadsheets to make decisions for you, instead of using the data to inform your decisions. Things can go badly wrong if managers outsource their decision making to the data in front of them.

Several years ago the pharmaceutical company Roche produced a drug called Accutane, which was a cure for acne. I am not talking about the routine acne of adolescence, but rather the severe, intractable, disfiguring acne that can persist into adulthood. Really medically serious acne, in other words.

However, Accutane had severe side effects. The suicide rate among those taking the drug was double that of the general population. That risk was particularly serious because the suicide rate among people with severe acne is already higher.

The drug could also cause irritable bowel disease. IBD can lead to Crohn's disease. Some Crohn's sufferers eventually have parts of their colons surgically removed. Unlucky patients end up with colostomy bags. The drug was approved for sale even though Roche knew of a study that showed 21.6% of Accutane patients experienced gastrointestinal side effects while taking the drug.

In the drug's packaging for patients, Roche included a warning that "less than 1% of patients" suffered bowel problems when they took it.

Over the years, more than 7,000 Accutane users sued Roche when they suffered from those side effects. One of those users was James Marshall, an actor who starred in *A Few Good Men* alongside Jack Nicholson and Tom Cruise. Another was Charles Bishop, who killed himself by deliberately crashing a Cessna airplane into the 28th floor of the Bank of America Building in Tampa, Florida, after he took the drug.

The company began to lose courtroom verdicts, and juries awarded the patients and their families millions in damages.

By 2009, after 18 years on the market, Roche stopped making Accutane.

Why wasn't Roche able to see the trouble brewing?

THE QUANT FALLACY

The answer, according to lawsuits that uncovered evidence in the Accutane cases, is that Roche's staff had a particular way of handling data generated by incoming reports of side-effect problems. They compared the incoming cases with the total number of Accutane prescriptions Roche had sold. That process vastly understated the problem with Accutane because most people don't report unpleasant side effects to drug companies—they simply stop taking the drug. Roche also had an internal algorithm that downgraded some complaints to doubtful.

The result was that when Roche compared the number of problems with the total number of prescriptions on the market, the problems did not appear to be statistically significant. And, to be fair, Roche didn't do anything legally wrong. By 2018, most of the Accutane lawsuits came to an end when Roche won its appeals on the basis that it had followed the Food and Drug Administration's regulations to the letter.

A normal person, who is not a data analyst, might have asked three common-sense questions: If this drug is so safe, why do people who take it kill themselves more often? Why do they end up with terrible bowel conditions that require surgery? And are these reasonable risks to treat a non-life-threatening condition like acne?

But at Roche, in my opinion, the data made the decisions: As long as the data said the problems were not statistically significant, Roche assumed it did not have a problem. This is what I call the quant fallacy. *Quant* is a nickname often given to quantitative data analysts who live and die by their spreadsheets. Quants tend to see the world as if it is fully encapsulated by the data they have gathered. Of course, the world is never fully captured by your data.

That's the quant fallacy: There's a difference between having good data and *applying judgment* to good data. That's your job: to apply judgment.

TEN-SECOND CHEAT SHEET

◔ Don't let the data make decisions for you.

◔ Don't become dependent on data produced by others. You won't know if they are making mistakes or measuring the wrong things, and thereby infecting your data with their errors. Generate and check your own data.

◔ Too much data can be as bad as too little. Focus on the core metrics that get the most results and ignore the rest.

◔ Beware the quant fallacy: There's a difference between having good data and applying judgment to good data. Don't outsource your judgment to the data.

◔ That's your job: to apply judgment.

III

PEOPLE

III
PEOPLE

11

Org charts and how I learned I was totally wrong to hate them

MOST companies won't ask you to climb through a glass case filled with tarantulas. But there is one company that has asked employees to do that: Zappos, the online shoe retailer.

At its quarterly all-hands meeting in 2013, multiple glass cases filled with spiders were pushed onto the stage at the Smith Center for Performing Arts in Las Vegas. An announcer then told employees that anyone willing to enter the tarantula boxes would win a $250 corporate gift card. One woman—dressed in a leopard costume, it's not clear why—took the dare. She won the money and was uninjured by the challenge, according to Aimee Groth's book about the company, *The Kingdom of Happiness*.

The next year, Zappos did something even stranger, as far as many staff were concerned. The CEO announced that he was abolishing the company's traditional management structure and replacing it with something called "Holacracy." The new system promised a radical self-governing "flatness." Many managers found their roles were essentially abolished. Instead of the corporate ladder, there were "no job titles, no managers, no hierarchy," as Groth has described it. The intention behind the super-flat structure was to give employees the freedom and the power to grow to their full potential, rather than waiting for the managers to promote them.

Holacracy plunged the company into confusion. Some staffers found themselves stewing in five extra hours of meetings per week just to figure out how Holacracy worked. It made many people miserable, according to *The Wall Street Journal*.

Crucially, there was a way to measure this misery: Zappos had an annual policy which offered three months' severance pay to any employee who wanted to leave. In a normal year, between 1% and 3% of employees took advantage of it, the *WSJ* said. But in 2015, Zappos reported that 14% of its staff—210 people out of about 1,500 in total—took the exit package.

After a couple more years, Zappos began quietly backing away from Holacracy, Groth reported later.

For years I also maintained a visceral hatred for "org charts"— the family-tree diagrams that show who is the boss of whom inside any given company. But then I heard about the chaos at Zappos. And that was when I realised my hatred of org charts had been wrong.

Clearly, not having one can create chaos.

USE THE RULE OF FIVE IN YOUR ORG CHART

At the start of this book, I noted that supervising a team of just three people feels effortless. It's easy to stay on the same page when you only have two other people to talk to.

But once you are managing more than five people—the rule of five—complications begin to kick in. You're in danger of crossing the threshold of dysfunction.

So you want a management structure that splits teams into units of five or fewer if possible, and gives the managers above them five or fewer direct reports if possible. Ideally, you want to end up with a structure that looks a lot like a pyramid, with bundles of workers in groups of three to five reporting to each boss, and these bosses reporting in groups of up to five to the bosses above them, and so on.

DELEGATION: THE EXISTENTIAL CRISIS OF MANAGEMENT

The only way to make this work is for you, the manager, to give up a lot of day-to-day responsibility and delegate heavily to the people reporting to you.

This will feel incredibly difficult at first.

Delegation necessitates a conceptual contradiction that managers can never quite resolve: the existential crisis of management. You are not doing the actual work. If you are running a factory or a restaurant, you are no longer physically making products or cooking meals. Instead, you're asking other people to do that work, but you're the one who remains responsible and accountable for the quality of the work being done. (To complicate things further, supervising the actual work is actually a lot of work!)

You have probably been promoted because you were good at your job. But managing others is a new and separate skill. You are not doing your old job.

You have a new job. You're in management.

The good news is that people generally want more control and responsibility over their work anyway. No one likes micromanagement. So delegate, as much as you can.

TEN-SECOND CHEAT SHEET

⏱ You will definitely need an org chart. People want to know where they stand.

⏱ Remember the rule of five: It is difficult to directly supervise a team that is larger than five people.

⏱ For more senior managers who supervise managers beneath them, the rule of five (direct reports) still applies.

⏱ Any more than six direct reports risks turning a perfectly effective manager into a reactive "ticket-taker" whose time is entirely taken up by the questions and needs of her staff.

⏱ Delegate, a lot. In groups larger than five, you will have no other choice.

⏱ Your staff will expect you to be well organized. If you are not a Type-A personality—someone who is highly organized and goal focused—then just pretend to be one. Act like a Type A until it becomes a normal habit.

12

The Myers-Briggs test and why you absolutely should not use it

IMAGINE someone in your HR department showed up at your desk one day and asked you to respond to these weird statements:

- "You enjoy watching people argue."
- "Your mood can change very quickly."
- "You avoid making phone calls."
- "You have always been fascinated by what, if anything, happens after death."

It would be as if they suspected you might be a psychopath.

Why else would anyone enjoy "watching people argue"? (Note that they are not asking whether you enjoy having an argument but whether you enjoy *watching other people* have an argument. Creepy.)

And why might your HR department think you might be fascinated by death?

These are all questions from the Myers-Briggs Type Indicator test, a personality quiz used by thousands of employers worldwide. Myers-Briggs asks you a few dozen questions, like the ones above, and asks you to rate your answers on a scale. It then places you in

97

one of 16 personality categories. The categories measure you based on your relative propensity for the following traits:

- Extraversion or introversion
- Sensing or intuition
- Thinking or feeling
- Judging or perceiving

The eight categories are represented by initials (E, I, S, N, T, F, J, and P), and at the end you are diagnosed with a four-letter combo. Last time I took it, I registered as an "INTJ", which stands for Introverted, Intuitive, Thinking, and Judging. That allegedly makes me "innovative, independent, strategic, logical, reserved, insightful, and driven by my own original ideas to achieve improvements." In some tests, these personality types are given cool-sounding nicknames. Mine is the Mastermind or the Architect, depending on which website you read.

It's all very flattering.

But very few people who know me would describe me as a mastermind.

The Myers-Briggs test is so common you may already have taken it yourself. If so, you have likely received an equally flattering assessment of your personality. Because it turns out that all 16 categories in the Myers-Briggs are upbeat, positive, and have only good things to say about you. Myers-Briggs only delivers one type of result, in 16 sunny ways.

There is no way to take the Myers-Briggs test and discover, for instance, that you are a miserable, self-hating jerk who overcompensates for your inadequacies with petty vendettas against your colleagues. Which is strange, because it would be genuinely useful if Myers-Briggs were able to weed out people like that!

And yet, millions of times a year, corporate HR departments ask their employees these questions, and categorize their personalities based on the results. "More than 10,000 companies, 2,500 colleges and universities and 200 government agencies in the United States use the test," according to an investigation by *The Washington Post*. At one point 89 of the top Fortune 100 companies used it.

Companies use the test to create workplace training programs that, in theory, are best suited to your personality type. They also believe that knowing your colleagues' personality types will help you communicate better with them.

There's just one problem.

Myers-Briggs is bullshit.

It was invented in 1943 by the mystery novelist Katharine Cook Briggs and her daughter Isabel Briggs Myers, a bank clerk. Neither of them had any scientific training whatsoever. But they were fans of the work of the psychoanalyst Carl Jung who, in 1921, theorized that personalities could be divided into several basic types. However, this was just an idea. Jung never tested it, or proved it, or provided any evidence for it.

SHOCKINGLY BAD

Undaunted, Myers and Briggs developed the idea, turning it into a test featuring a series of bizarre questions that respondents are asked to agree or disagree with. The test was picked up by various government agencies and educational institutions, taking on a life of its own.

Since then dozens of scientists have pointed out that Myers-Briggs is pseudoscience. There is no peer-reviewed, statistically significant, double-blind research demonstrating that it works. *Scientific American* said Myers-Briggs was "one of the worst personality tests in existence for a wide range of reasons. It is unreliable because a person's type may change from day to day.

It gives false information ("bogus stuff," one researcher puts it). The questions are confusing and poorly worded."

Simine Vazire, a researcher at the University of California, Davis, has called it "shockingly bad."

Jung himself disowned the idea behind Myers-Briggs even though his work inspired it. "Every individual is an exception to the rule," Jung said. To "stick labels on people at first sight," he argued, was "nothing but a childish parlor game."

As a manager it may feel tempting to subject your staff to some kind of psychology test. It feels intuitively useful to know that Johnny is "playful and enthusiastic" whereas Mary is "action-oriented and logical." Maybe that information could help you communicate more effectively with them, if you can do so in their style? But at the end of the day, Mary and Johnny both have the same job. That project needs to be done by Friday, come hell or high water. The client doesn't care whether Johnny is an "ISFP" or Mary an "ENTJ."

That's why your ability as a communicator is more important than your ability as a psychoanalyst. It's why managing feels mostly like communicating—clearly, over and over again.

So, please, don't use Myers-Briggs on your staff.

TEN-SECOND CHEAT SHEET

- Human resources departments in thousands of companies worldwide use the Myers-Briggs Type Indicator test to tailor their workplace training and communication styles.

- Myers-Briggs will not help you communicate better with your staff. You should ignore it.

- The test was invented by a mystery novelist and a bank clerk. Neither had any scientific training.

- They were inspired by famous psychoanalyst Carl Jung, who disowned the idea.

- Actual scientists have debunked it and now regard Myers-Briggs as one of the worst personality categorisation tests.

- Even if Myers-Briggs did give you insight into your colleagues' personalities, the fact is that your success is more dependent on your ability to communicate successfully with them than your ability to see into their brains.

- Don't use Myers-Briggs if you can avoid it!

13

Hiring: Why soccer teams don't recruit their own fans

You probably don't know who Brad Katsuyama is.

Katsuyama was an executive at the Royal Bank of Canada who, a few years ago, noticed that whenever he tried to buy a large order of stock for a client, the price of the stock would shift upward right before he hit "buy" on his computer.

The system didn't feel honest. The stock prices displayed by the market were false. Every time Katsuyama tried to buy at the price on offer, the actual price shifted the second he made an order. At first he thought it was just a coincidence. But it happened time and time again, and he got spooked. Someone seemed to know exactly when he wanted to buy stock, and moved against him at exactly the right time. It was as if they were looking over his shoulder, watching the computer on which he was placing his trade, according to Michael Lewis's masterful account of the mystery in the book *Flash Boys*.

Katsuyama became determined to figure out what was going on. He asked around.

He discovered that the problem wasn't just with him. It was systemic. It cost RBC and its clients untold millions every year. Investment banks trade extremely large volumes of stock. Even if prices move by just a few pennies, millions are lost. Yet no one knew who was doing it, or how they were able to see bank trades before they were actually made.

Katsuyama wasn't the only one who was stumped.

Over at Goldman Sachs—one of the most prestigious investment banks on Wall Street—executives were also suspicious as to why the not-so-prestigious Morgan Stanley was doing better than they were in the stock trading business.

Morgan Stanley was trading 300m shares a day, or 30% of the New York Stock Exchange's volume. They made $500m a year from that business. Goldman, by contrast, controlled a paltry 8% of the market.

Both Katsuyama at RBC and Goldman employed the same technique in their attempt to find out how Morgan Stanley was beating them at their own game: They recruited for jobs at their companies, and invited dozens of executives from rival banks to apply for them. Katsuyama interviewed more than 100 rival people. Goldman targeted Morgan Stanley employees specifically and spoke to dozens.

Bank employees are often required to sign confidentiality contracts as a condition of their employment, so they are not supposed to tell anyone about their work. But in a conversation about a potential new job, people quickly forget all that. They are keen to describe the value of the work they do, how they do it, and why it's different to everyone else.

That was good news for Katsuyama and Goldman, because they were very interested in finding out how it was that other banks—especially Morgan Stanley—seemed to have a jump on all their trades.

HOW GOOD HIRING UNCOVERED A $14.4M
WALL STREET SCANDAL

Their detective work paid off. It turned out that rival banks had found a way to arbitrage the tiny differences in speed at which electronic purchase orders arrive on stock exchanges. Some investment banks had deployed software that was able to see Katsuyama's orders coming in before the rest of the market reacted. Then, in a fraction of a second, the system would buy the stock and sell it to Katsuyama at a higher price. The high-frequency trading programs were so fast they beat everyone, buying and selling before Goldman's and RBC's orders could be fulfilled.

They were front-running the market, and distorting stock prices in the process.

They were cheating, basically.

Katsuyama had uncovered a major scandal. Banks were breaking the law to cheat traders who didn't have access to high-speed trading algorithms. Hundreds of millions of dollars in stock trades were being manipulated by a handful of banks.

In 2015, UBS paid a $14.4m fine to the Securities and Exchange Commission to settle allegations that it was secretly front-running trades for a select group of investors who were clients of its "dark" high-frequency trading program.

This story is famous on Wall Street. *Flash Boys* is now being made into a movie. Lewis's main point is: *In job interviews, people will tell you anything*.

As a manager you should use this to your advantage.

A MAJOR ADVANTAGE OF ACTIVELY POACHING TALENT IS TO EDUCATE YOURSELF

People underestimate the usefulness of knowing what is going on elsewhere in your industry—especially at rival companies.

Talking to people you'd like to hire at other companies, even if they turn you down, is a good way to improve your knowledge of the hiring marketplace as a whole.

A tactic I highly recommend is to draw up a list of people at rival companies whom you would love to hire and then invite them out for coffee.

Smart people are flattered and open to outside offers, even if they aren't looking to move. Once you have pulled someone into a conversation about potential opportunities, you'll be surprised what you can learn.

You also want to spread good buzz about yourself and your company into rival companies. Let them know you are growing. Let them know you are hiring. Let them know you are succeeding and looking for new talent. Let them know your place is faster, more exciting, more interesting, and less filled with morons, than their office.

ALWAYS MAKE HIRING YOUR NO.1 PRIORITY

Your no.1 priority, always, should be to hire the best people you can, and promote the talent you want to keep.

If you learn nothing else from this book, know this: Hiring the right person for the right position will solve 80% of your problems. Remember, your challenge as a manager is that you are no longer doing the actual hands-on work. (Or at least, you're probably doing less of it.) Certainly, if you are supervising others, you are relying on the quality and speed of their work. If things go wrong, it's on you. If things go right, you get credit. So you absolutely need to care about the calibre of people on your team. It doesn't matter how good a manager you are; if the people underneath you are incompetent, you will never succeed.

Therefore, you should devote as much time to hiring the best people you possibly can.

As long as you know that, you can throw the rest of this book away and you will probably be OK as a manager.

BAD HIRING: WHY SOCCER TEAMS DON'T ADVERTISE THEIR JOB VACANCIES

At many companies (particularly bad companies), hiring is an essentially passive process in which the company advertises its vacancies and generates a constant stream of incoming applications from hopeful job candidates. Then the managers (particularly bad managers) look through those applications and try to choose the best ones.

This is a pretty good way to end up with some mediocre people on your team.

Think about it this way: Why is a professional soccer team—like, say, Liverpool FC—better than your office soccer team?

There are many reasons, obviously. But a key difference is how they approach recruitment. Your office team is restricted to choosing its players only from those who volunteer to show up.

At a professional sports franchise, no one chooses from the people who volunteer to show up. Even if Liverpool chose its players from among all the club's fans—millions of people worldwide, no doubt some very good players among them—they wouldn't get a set of players as good as the ones currently on the pitch.

Professional teams don't passively choose from the volunteers. Instead, they spend most of their recruitment time actively trying to poach players from rival teams, or looking at younger players at lower-flight clubs who are promising enough to warrant a promotion.

Their recruitment is highly targeted and specific. They have great knowledge of rivals in the marketplace and they look for individuals with specific skills. They call them on the phone. They ask to meet them. They will spend months or years maintaining a relationship with a player until he is ready to move to a new team.

The one thing they *don't* do is look through piles of emails from fans who'd love to be given a chance at Anfield.

I am not saying that people who apply to your job vacancy ads are bad applicants. Certainly, you have to advertise your vacancies. I have hired plenty of excellent people who applied for a job based on the ads we posted. But if you are *only* passively choosing from whoever walks through your door, you won't get the staff you need to excel.

You need to do more.

HIRING FOR DIVERSITY, EQUITY, AND INCLUSION

There is a myth among managers that hiring should be purely meritocratic. This myth says that if you simply hire "the best," four things will happen:

- The results of your hiring will be fair.
- You will get the best people regardless of their background.
- A selection of only the best people will include many Black, Asian, minority, ethnic, disabled, and LGBT staffers because you are selecting for *talent* not *background*.
- Thus your hiring will be diverse.

I used to believe this, but I became suspicious of it when I saw how it panned out in real life. When I first began sifting through resumés among the applications for jobs at Insider, I was (obviously) looking for the best people. So I looked at candidates who graduated from the best-known universities and colleges: Ivy League schools, and Oxford and Cambridge in the UK. Those institutions are highly competitive and difficult to get into. They must, therefore, be producing the best—right?

Over time I came to realize that, if I wanted to, I could fill every job vacancy we had with candidates from these colleges. Many companies do, in fact, hire precisely this way. Goldman Sachs and other investment banks pull heavily from Ivy League institutions. Likewise, in the UK, *The Guardian*, the BBC, and *The Times* notoriously prefer hires from Oxford and Cambridge.

Yet Oxford and Cambridge's system for selecting students has a major flaw. They are not, actually, selecting for the best people.

Here is how it works.

Oxford and Cambridge—and many of the Ivy League campuses—prefer to take in the best high-school students as undergraduates. Unfortunately, their definition of "best" has historically meant taking a disproportionate number of students from a small number of elite private secondary schools.

Most teenagers, obviously, do not go to private school. Private school is expensive. Most people are not rich enough to afford it. In the UK, 94% of people are educated in the state-funded school system. A mere 6% of kids go to private schools.

Yet, in 2019 only 49% of Oxford's places went to state-school students. The majority went to private school students from the UK or international students from foreign countries. And guess what type of schools international students come from? That's right: 95% of Oxford's international students went to private school, according to a sample of admission numbers published by *Cherwell*, the Oxford student newspaper.

The problem with this, of course, is that there is a high correlation between being rich and being white. Between 2012 and 2016 some Cambridge colleges admitted zero Black people, according to an investigation by the *Financial Times*. Zero—meaning none at all.

In 2016 Oxford only took in 35 Black students out of a student body of 2,210, according to research done by my Insider colleague Lindsay Dodgson. By 2020 that number had risen to 106. That's still an astonishingly small number, especially given that you might reasonably expect the international students to be less white than British students. (In fairness to Oxford and Cambridge, they have begun making their admissions more fair in recent years. In 2020 53.2% of admissions were from state schools. But that is still far below 93%, the portion of students in state schools.)

The situation is similar at Ivy League universities—they have a selection bias in favor of private school candidates and the children of their successful alumni.

Clearly, any employer who is using Oxbridge or Ivy League as a proxy signal for "best" candidates will end up selecting staff not on the basis of talent but on the basis of wealth. In turn, that is going to give you an office full of white people.

I am not saying "never hire from the elite colleges." Rather, I am saying *their* criteria should not be *your* criteria, and thus you need to look a little further afield to find the people who are perfect for the business you are running.

That's why you should recruit people using a variety of methods. You certainly want to look at the best people who applied through your recruitment ads. But you should also actively target people you want to recruit, like a football team manager. If you only rely on your help-wanted ads, that could give you all the flaws baked into a system that discriminates against people who aren't white or aren't wealthy enough to go to private school.

You're going to need to work harder to get the best people—and that involves actively reaching out to the people you want, not simply waiting for them to show up on their own.

HOW BAD HIRING MADE CAMERAS RACIST

There are other advantages to hiring from as diverse a field of talent as possible, aside from it being merely the right thing to do.

You want a wide range of people among your staff because you want a wide range of perspectives to inform the work you are doing. You don't know everything. But you can broaden your available knowledge by having a range of different types of people in your workforce, at all levels. That on its own is likely to make your team collectively smarter, and there is value in that.

It will also help prevent you from making mistakes—mistakes you don't even know you might be making.

Perhaps the most infamous example of a huge corporate failure based on lack of diversity comes from Kodak. In the days before digital cameras, Kodak produced the best-selling camera film on the planet. Color reproduction from film has to be calibrated so that the chemicals on the film correctly reproduce the colors and tones the camera is pointed at. Starting in the mid-1950s, Kodak used a test card to get those color reproductions just right. The test card featured a model whose name was Shirley. Shirley was beautiful. She had big 1950s hair, and was often depicted wearing an off-the-shoulder evening dress or opera gloves. The test was simple: If Shirley's skin looked good then the camera film was correctly calibrated. If Shirley looked weird then something was off with the film.

The problem was that Shirley was white. There were no test cards featuring Black, Asian or any other ethnicity of Shirleys. So camera film became calibrated to perfectly reproduce white skin, not Black or brown skin. Different skin colors reflect light at different levels, so calibrating for only the lightest kind of skin skewed the film's performance to one end of the scale.

If you have ever wondered why historic photographs of dark-skinned people never seem to look as good as those of white people, this is the reason: Film was only optimized for one of the races.

The Shirley cards were used for decades, and their effect became infamous among professionals who struggled to take pictures of non-white people that looked good. Jean-Luc Godard, perhaps the most famous French film director of all time, declared Kodak's film to be racist in 1977, and he refused to use it on a shoot in Mozambique.

DIGITAL CAMERAS CAN BE RACIST TOO

Unbelievably (or perhaps not, given the history), the camera industry reproduced the same error when calibrating facial recognition software in the digital cameras on our phones and those used in closed-circuit security camera systems.

Digital cameras use software to recognize faces in order to auto-focus the camera on the face of anyone you are taking a picture of. Facial recognition software is also used for security and law-enforcement purposes.

But to make sure the software works correctly, it first has to be calibrated, and that requires "training" the software. The training consists of running thousands of sample photos through the software's algorithm until it has enough examples to correctly predict what it is looking at. Unfortunately, the data sets of sample photos used by the digital camera industry feature an abundance of white people and disproportionately few Black people. One standard data set is 77% male and 83% white, according to the researchers Timnit Gebru and Joy Buolamwini.

Gebru and Buolamwini found one camera algorithm had only a 0.8% error rate when it was asked to identify white men. But the error rate went up to 34% for minority women.

This is why digital cameras sometimes fail to take good pictures of brown-skinned people. Worse, it is also why facial recognition technology is good at identifying white people but bad at identifying Black people.

Clearly, if you are in the camera business and you are boasting about the accuracy of your products, these are embarrassing failures. Failures that, perhaps, would not have occurred had the teams and managers creating these products featured more people who were not white.

It's not that the camera industry is filled with racists deliberately making cameras that don't work for people of color. It's that their photography staff didn't include anyone who, decades ago, could have said, "Hey, maybe we need to calibrate this stuff for everyone, not just for Shirley."

Diverse teams have more information available to them, from more perspectives, and so they tend to be more innovative. This diversity-innovation nexus pays benefits: Diverse teams generate 19% more revenue than non-diverse teams, on average, according to a Boston Consulting Group study of 1,700 companies in eight countries from 2017.

So if you want your teams to be successful, you must actively hire for diversity.

TEN-SECOND CHEAT SHEET

- Hiring good people is the most important activity you can do as a manager. Always make it your No.1 priority.

- Tell talented people elsewhere that you are interested in having them come work for you.

- Use job interviews to learn more about rival employers and to promote your reputation in the marketplace.

- Use job interviews to find out who else the candidate might know who might want to work for you.

- Use job interviews to spread the word in your industry that you are hiring and people should get in touch.

- Hire for diversity. You will get better results and make fewer mistakes.

14

How to hire people who are better than you

HEATHER was the managing editor of a monthly magazine in New York that covered the fashion and design world. It was one of those glossy books where the readership was measured more by its influence than its size. Her job was to hire interns and entry-level staff.

One candidate she spoke to had been born and raised in the West Village of Manhattan, and she very much wanted Heather to know this in the job interview. She felt it made her more cosmopolitan and sophisticated than the other candidates. New York was the center of the world, she argued, and the funky, bohemian West Village was its diverse and teeming heart. If she could handle life in the big bad city, she could handle anything.

This struck Heather as odd. Manhattan is a 24/7 city. Everything your heart might desire is within walking distance—even in the middle of the night. Surely, living in Manhattan might be easier than living elsewhere?

So Heather asked her to describe a time when the candidate faced adversity in her life, and how she got through it.

She thought for a bit. And then she told Heather this:

After high school she accepted a place at the University of Massachusetts. But in the first semester a huge snowstorm swept across the state. New England winters can be brutal. The snow fell so thickly it cut the power to her student dormitory hall. The streets were blocked. For three days, the students were snowed in, cut off from the outside world.

Sounds like a bad storm, Heather thought. But they were first-year students trapped in their dorms: Surely they turned it into a party? Mass snowball fights? Some kind of snow-tunnelling adventure?

Nope!

When the weather improved, the woman called her parents, dropped out of UMass, and enrolled in New York University— steps from the apartment she grew up in.

Heather did not hire this person. Bailing on your colleagues because of bad weather is not a solution. And Heather didn't want to work with someone whose idea of solving a problem is giving up and going home.

I like Heather's story because it touches on a truth: Sometimes work is difficult. Sometimes it's not fun. You can only get through those times if you are working with people who are prepared to push through adversity.

Here are the general principles I work from when looking at candidates for a job:

CREATE A STANDARD PACKAGE REQUIRED FROM ALL JOB OR PROMOTION APPLICANTS

You should ask job candidates for three things:

- Their LinkedIn account.
- Five examples of their best work.
- A timed test in which they pitch you ideas about your industry.

That will give you three different pieces of comparable information on which to judge every candidate. By making everyone do the same thing—and the great thing about LinkedIn is that it makes everyone's résumés look identical—it becomes easier to see who stands out from the crowd.

It is also good to treat all applicants equally for legal and ethical reasons.

ARE THEY BETTER THAN ME?

You may be tempted to assume that you are a manager because you are the best person at your job and no one can ever do it better. This is a ridiculous idea.

You actually want to hire people who are better at this than you are. Remember, as a manager you're doing less and less of the actual work and more and more of the organizing of the work. So you're going to need people on your teams who are the best.

A simple way to drive up the average quality of your teams is to make sure that whenever someone leaves, you replace them with someone better, not someone with the same level of skill. Every new hire you make should increase the average level of talent on your team. You can start by only hiring people who are better at the job than you.

David Ogilvy, founder of the ad agency Ogilvy & Mather, famously said, "If each of us hires people who are smaller than we are, we shall become a company of dwarfs. But if each of us hires people who are bigger than we are, we shall become a company of giants."

HOW TO RECRUIT DIVERSELY

I made the case in the previous chapter that passively advertising your vacancies and picking the "best" from whoever responds will not actually get you the best people—and may also generate racist results. So you're going to need a recruitment strategy to counter that, because it is likely that a lot of your company's recruitment is going to come from advertising vacancies.

Good companies have a program of outreach to any and all professional organisations that represent minority professionals in their field. Their senior managers are continuously making phone calls to professionals of color to introduce themselves, to encourage people to look at their job vacancies, and to directly recruit minority candidates for open roles. They do this in addition to passively advertising their jobs. This is time-consuming (it's easier to sift piles of incoming résumés, after all). But it is a way of discovering talent you may previously have overlooked. And if you believe that hiring the right people is 80% of everything, then having additional sources of new talent becomes a competitive advantage.

There are also a few tricks you can incorporate into your hiring process to weed out elite college bias. I have interviewed executives at hundreds of companies over the years. Lots of them are trying to widen and diversify their hiring processes as they recruit new talent. Here are some of the best ideas they told me:

- **Offer a test:** Ask applicants to take a test rather than looking at résumés. A person's university degree tells you very little about their actual ability to do the job you are recruiting for, so why not have applicants take a test for the job instead? You could ask applicants to pitch you five new ideas your company might pursue. It's a great way to see how people think about your business.
- **Inclusive shortlists:** By insisting that the shortlist for all

jobs must include people of color, members of the LGBT community, and/or people with disabilities, you can force your recruiters and managers to look at the widest field of talent available, and not simply those who are best connected to the company.

- **Use name-blind résumés:** People's names often give away their ethnicity and generate stereotypes in your head before you've had the chance to evaluate them objectively. So one way to change your application process is to prevent people from writing their name in their application and give them a code number instead.

- **Remove university names:** Some investment banks have started removing names of colleges and universities from job applications. You'll be able to see that a person has a degree in economics, for instance, but you won't know if it was from Harvard or Rutgers—thus forcing you to judge them on their actual merits, in theory.

AFTER THAT, SORT FOR THE BEST CANDIDATES

Here are the qualities I look for:

- **Crankers:** A characteristic you should look for is someone who can do a lot of work very quickly, and is excited about the idea of a company that moves at speed. Crankers tend to accomplish a lot more than others.

- **Builders:** I also look for people who like the idea of building a successful new team or product from scratch, making it bigger and more impressive month after month. Some people show up at work and just do the job. But others want to build something new and like the idea of taking on that responsibility. Look for the builders. A good mix of builders and crankers is invaluable.

- **People who campaign to get in:** You want to hire people who want to work for you, and when you look through a great many candidates, you will notice that some of them want to work at your company specifically. The work *you* do is the work *they* want to do. They apply for more than one job at the company. Maybe they have emailed you directly with extra pitches or proposals. Sometimes these candidates ask for feedback on why you rejected them—because they want to know how to succeed next time. In general, you should sort in favor of this positive trait.

- **Filter out the people who just want a job:** The one type of candidate you definitely do not want to hire is the person who "just wants a job."

  There is nothing wrong with wanting to work, or needing to work, of course. But the "just want a job" people see work as that thing you do between 9 a.m. and 5 p.m. in order to pay the rent. They don't see it as their life's passion, as a set of ladders that will build a career they can be proud of. They are less likely to go above and beyond the call of duty. As a manager, you want to create teams that are above-average performers, and that means finding people who will go the extra mile because they know that's how you succeed.

  You won't get that from people who just want a job.

MY FAVORITE JOB INTERVIEW QUESTIONS

I have a handful of favorite questions I like to ask in interviews. A common theme in these questions is that they help you filter out the people you definitely do not want to hire: People who just want a job. My favorite question is based on the story of the candidate who couldn't handle a snowstorm:

- **"What was the most difficult project you ever tackled at work? Tell me how you handled it."** You get a wide range of answers to this—and those answers can give you real insight into a person's work ethic. Very often, you find that some people's idea of a difficult task is something that you regard as routine or trivial. You want to hire people who have tackled genuinely challenging work projects. People who know what hard work looks like, essentially.
- **"What do you really want to achieve in your career? What is your dream job?"** This question—sometimes phrased as "Where do you see yourself in five years' time?"—sounds cheesy, but the answer ought to give you insight into whether this person really wants the job you are offering or simply wants a job to pay the rent. Is this job exactly what they want? Will they use the job to push forward their career in a relevant and useful way? In other words, are they going to take the role you are offering and build it into something even bigger?
- **"What do you think we do poorly? What could use improvement?"** This question essentially tests whether they actually know about your company and whether they have done some research about what you do before applying for the job. You will also get some interesting and occasionally useful answers about aspects of your work that could be improved. If a candidate gives an ignorant answer to this question, you know that they don't really know much about your company.
- **"What is the most interesting issue in your field of work right now, and why?"** You want to look for people who

know about your field, follow it, and have a passion for it. If you get an interesting and original answer to this question, that's a positive. You want to filter out the people whose answers betray their ignorance of your industry.

- **"Why did you leave your last employer (or any previous employer)?"** Smart candidates know that complaining about their old (or current) boss is never a good look in a job interview, but many do this anyway. You also get an idea of whether this person is a complainer who engages in personal drama or whether they are just looking for a new challenge.

ASKING FOR REFERENCES

On the face of it, asking prospective job candidates for references—people who will recommend hiring them and be willing to answer questions as to why—is insane.

No one is going to list a referee who will say bad things about them. But there are a handful of questions you can ask in a reference call that will help you see what a candidate's good and bad points might be. (And, just like job interviews, this is another opportunity to extract information from people who work at rival companies.)

Here is a list of my favorite reference questions:

- **"Tell me how you know this person, and how long you have known them?"** Really basic question, right? The reason I ask this is I want to know whether the referee knows this person well or not. And I also want to know whether they have actually worked with the candidate. You'd be surprised how many people list their friends as referees. There is nothing wrong with that, of course. But being someone's friend is not the same as working alongside them.

- **"What are this candidate's strengths?"** This is a softball question but you need to get the conversation going somehow!
- **"What are this candidate's weak spots?"** Everyone has holes in their game. You might as well find out what these are before you hire them. It is also interesting to compare the referee's answer to the candidate's answer to the same question in the job interview.
- **"If the candidate doesn't work out in this job, why might that be?"** This is a great question because it is very difficult to answer with fluffy, positive spin. The answers to this question often turn on a candidate's negative character traits.
- **"Describe the most difficult project this candidate took on, and tell me how she handled it."** This is another analog of the question you asked in the job interview. I like this question because it elicits an incredibly wide range of answers.
- **"What does this candidate really want to achieve in her career?"** Again, you asked a similar question of the candidate during the job interview. I like to ask the referees too because it shows you the difference between the way the candidate perceives herself and the actual message she has given to people in her network.

TEN-SECOND CHEAT SHEET

⏱ Hire people who don't flake when faced with adversity or difficulty.

- ⏱ Create a standard package of materials required from all job candidates.

- ⏱ Look for people who are better at this than you. Every new hire should increase the average talent level of the team.

- ⏱ Recruit for diversity to make sure you are getting the best people.

- ⏱ Hiring for diversity requires extra work—you will not get the best talent by passively advertising your vacancies.

- ⏱ Use the bag of tricks detailed in this chapter to level the playing field among your applicants and highlight their actual talent as opposed to the luck of their birthright.

- ⏱ Look for crankers.

- ⏱ Look for builders.

- ⏱ Look for people who campaign to get in.

- ⏱ Filter out the people who just want a job.

- ⏱ Use a list of questions like the ones in this chapter to guide your job interviews.

- ⏱ Do the same thing when questioning their referees.

- ⏱ Take notes during job interviews—otherwise you will forget what you liked about them, and what their weaknesses were.

- ⏱ Take all new hires to lunch on their first day at work with you. This makes people feel welcome. It is a lot easier to work with people who feel welcomed onto your team. It's also a good opportunity—less formal, more casual—for them to ask you questions about what it is like working for you.

15

The Van Halen test:
Who you should promote

THE rock band Van Halen—whose hits include "Jump" and "Panama"—used to make concert venues sign an infamous tour contract, which included a demand for a backstage bowl of M&Ms candy with all the brown ones removed. The language in the rider, one line of type among hundreds, asks for various "Munchies," including potato chips with assorted dips, nuts, and pretzels. And then it said:

"M&M's (WARNING: ABSOLUTELY NO BROWN ONES)."

Most people concluded that the "no brown M&Ms" demand was simply a symptom of the colossal egos of the band members. They would cancel gigs at the last minute if they discovered brown M&Ms on their dressing-room buffet tables. "No brown M&Ms" became a well-known joke about the band.

Years later, lead singer David Lee Roth explained why the band had this ridiculous demand. It was a test of whether the managers at smaller concert venues were paying attention to detail and safety.

"We'd pull up with nine eighteen-wheeler trucks, full of gear, where the standard was three trucks, max. And there were many,

many technical errors—whether it was the girders couldn't support the weight, or the flooring would sink in, or the doors weren't big enough to move the gear through," he wrote in his autobiography.

"Van Halen was the first to take 850 par lamp lights—huge lights—around the country," Roth said later, in a 2012 interview. "At the time it was the biggest production ever." Not all venues were prepared. "If I came backstage, having been one of the architects of this lighting and stage design, and I saw brown M&Ms on the catering table, then I guarantee the promoter had not read the contract rider, and we would have to do a serious line check."

People's lives were at stake: It's easy to kill someone if a huge piece of lighting rig, dangling above the stage, falls because someone didn't get the details right when they set it up.

THE HIDDEN VALUE OF RELIABILITY

I first heard the rumor about Van Halen and the brown M&Ms in my first proper media job, at *The Register Citizen*, the daily newspaper for Torrington, Connecticut.

Torrington is a typical small American town. Its main street is literally called Main Street. It has a population of about 40,000. It sits in a small valley surrounded by trees. Its older houses are of the classic New England style—Victorian clapboards with shutters and gables of the kind you read about in Stephen King novels. Historically, the dominant employer was an old tool factory. The local hospital probably had more employees by the time I lived there. But Torrington regarded itself as a historic, rust-belt milltown, so the tool factory was a larger part of its blue-collar identity.

The Register Citizen had a venerable history as a family-owned paper going back to 1874. It had a staff of about 25 people in the newsroom—before the internet decimated the local newspaper business. The paper, in its day, was the heart of the community.

I had one important task in my first role as a copy editor at *The Register Citizen*: to bring back everyone's coffee and donut orders from the local café, called Talk of the Town.

I did this pretty much every day for about six months. You could argue it was demeaning. I was supposed to be editing a daily newspaper. But I was fetching the coffee.

Nonetheless, the Van Halen Rule applied: I noticed that when someone else did the coffee run and got the orders wrong, the senior editors on the desk would subject them to five minutes of joshing about their incompetence. People can be fussy about their coffee! No one ever just wants "a coffee." They want their coffee *just so*.

Fetching coffee and donuts without making mistakes is a pretty good way to demonstrate that you are reliable enough to be trusted with tasks that require zero errors.

By the end of the year they did trust me. I was placed in charge of editing the front page. It was my job to pick the stories, write the headlines, and select the photos that everyone would see on the street the next day. At the weekend, that meant being in sole charge of the whole paper. When news broke late at night, it was my job to run into the print room at the back of the building—where the newspaper was being printed at high speed on giant rollers—and yell "Stop the presses!" Just like in the movies.

It was a dream job for a new journalist. I was never a great newspaper editor. But I got that promotion because I got the job done and made few mistakes.

YOU'LL BE SURPRISED AT THE NUMBER OF EMPLOYEES WHO ARE NOT GREAT AT FOLLOWING INSTRUCTIONS

When you are considering promoting someone, reliability turns out to have enormous value.

As a manager, you are relying on others to complete your work. So knowing who can be trusted to get the job done—and who cannot—is one of the most important factors when you are considering a promotion for somebody.

This is an aspect of managing people that, frankly, came as a big surprise to me. Some people are just not great at doing what they are told. I don't mean they are insubordinate or incompetent. It is more subtle than that. They're just not great at completing a task.

I used to be one of them.

THAT TIME I COVERED MYSELF IN INDUSTRIAL GLUE

My first job as an adult was as a delivery driver for a cardboard box factory. I drove truckloads of our products—big stacks of boxes and giant barrels of glue—to our customers in the Northwest of England. The truck they gave me was the largest type available for someone who did not have a heavy-goods-vehicle license: It weighed a little over eight tons. It had a raised cab, so it was just like driving a "real" freight lorry. The truck also had much poorer visibility than a regular car. There was no central rearview mirror— the cargo hold prevented that. I was entirely dependent on the wing mirrors. That meant it was impossible to see the back wheels of the truck from the driver's seat.

Crucially, it was eight meters in length. This meant I had to take the corners and the curves exceptionally wide. If you don't take the corners wide, you drag your back wheels over the curbs, bumping and jostling the cargo hold. Failure to take wide turns can pull down traffic posts. You can even kill pedestrians.

I was a bad truck driver. When I drove my truck, new dents and scratches were daily occurrences. I routinely pulled the branches off trees with the back of the wagon. I once lost a wing mirror because I drove too close to a hedge in a country lane. I damaged this truck every single time I drove it.

Every. Single. Time.

On my worst day, I failed to secure a load of barrels I was delivering to a well-known chemical company in Liverpool. The barrels were filled with glue. Halfway through the journey, after my back wheels had bumped over a half-dozen curbs I had failed to take wide enough, I heard the barrels get loose and start rolling around in the back, banging into the walls and doors. Each barrel weighed about a ton: Too heavy for me to lift on my own. There was nothing I could do until I got to the client's delivery dock, where there would be a forklift that would help me wrestle the barrels back onto the wooden pallet they should have been tied to.

I got to the factory, reversed my truck into the loading dock, and then tried to open the back door. It was stuck. It just would not roll up.

I was horrified.

I knew the barrels were loose in the back, but now I suspected that the glue might have leaked—and glued the door shut during the journey.

The guys in the factory were laughing their heads off. I yanked and yanked at the back door. Suddenly it gave way, rattling upward into its shutter.

Immediately, a tidal wave of white glue—about 300 gallons from each barrel—poured out of the back of the lorry right onto my legs. I was covered in the stuff.

More laughter.

Much of the cargo was lost. I had to be hosed down outdoors, like an animal, before I could get back into the truck and drive it home. I was the worst truck driver in history. I just couldn't do a single day's driving without an expensive mishap.

There will be someone like me on your team.

Do not promote this person.

THE EXECUTION PROBLEM

This is what I call the execution problem.

Some workers, frankly, can't get through the day without intervention from their bosses or colleagues. That's OK at the junior levels of the company, as long as they are learning and improving over time. Everyone makes mistakes. But in terms of a promotion or a new hire, you really want people who can just get the job done without your help.

You will see this pattern emerge quickly. There will be folks on your team who get stuff done—no mess, no fuss. And then you have a small number of employees who can't seem to do anything without the frequent assistance of colleagues.

Some people are good at executing. Others are not. Obviously, you want to promote the executors on your staff, and to encourage them to recruit people who, similarly, are good at getting stuff done.

But you need to look for other qualities as well.

- **Low drama:** Look around at the people you work with. Who is getting the most work done, most successfully? You especially want to identify people who are doing a lot of successful work *quietly*. Not literally in silence, of course. But with the minimum amount of fuss. These people are worth their weight in gold. They are difficult to replace. You want to promote the low-drama people.

- **High productivity:** This is easy to notice. Who is getting most done around here? These people are keepers.
- **Right first time:** Can this person get it right the first time, all the time? Occasional mistakes are OK. We all make them. But the people you want to promote should be the folks whose work is consistently perfect the first time around, not the ones who cannot get there without help. Some people say "consistency is the hobgoblin of little minds" but they are wrong about this. In the world of work—or anything else you want to be successful at—consistency is the hobgoblin of excellence.
- **Crankers and builders:** Of course, you are looking for the same qualities in new hires.

LADDERS FOR ROCK STARS

Let's imagine you work in sales. The skills you need to succeed as a salesperson are something like these: You're good at cold-calling. You're good at pitching. You don't easily become downcast when people tell you no. At the end of the process the client feels happy to have met you, and not ripped off. Let's imagine that you are the best salesperson in your office.

Who should management promote to become the office director?

Most companies would tap you for the job—because you are the best—and you'd happily accept the promotion. But managing people requires a completely different set of skills to making sales. Managing doesn't usually involve a lot of cold-calling, for instance.

So the irony is that when companies promote their best workers, they lose their best workers. Notoriously, people who are great at sales are often terrible managers.

It's the same in sports. No one ever takes their top goal-scorer off the field and promotes her to coach. It's better if she stays on the pitch and continues to knock them into the back of the net.

Not everyone should go into management. Some people are good at their jobs and should stay in those jobs. But those people probably don't want to feel that their careers are stagnating. So it is worth creating ladders for rock stars who are not managers.

In other words, you should create a two-track promotion system:

- One for those heading into management who are actually good at organizing and leading other people.
- The other for rock stars who may not be good as managers, but who nevertheless want meaningful career growth.

The people on the rock-star ladder should be able to earn a series of ever-escalating prestigious job titles, with increasing pay, even though they may not be supervising anyone. If their work is great and you need them to stay, reward them for it even if they are not on the management track.

Remember, people who are good at their jobs don't want to stagnate. They want to feel like they are climbing up the ladder too.

TEN-SECOND CHEAT SHEET

When considering who to promote, look for:

- ⬡ Reliability.

- ⬡ People who can execute.

- ⬡ People who are low drama.

- ⬡ People who are highly productive.

- ⬡ People who are crankers.

- ⬡ People who are builders.

- ⬡ People who get it right first time. Consistency is the hobgoblin of excellence.

- ⬡ Build ladders for rock stars: Make a separate promotion track to recognize the rock stars who don't supervise anyone.

- ⬡ Tell your star players that they are stars. Tell them that you have big plans, and that they should stick around to reap the rewards. They will be less likely to defect to the competition if they believe their future is bright with you. (Of course, you actually have to deliver on your big plans and the rewards that go with them.)

16

Managing up:
The monkey on
your back

THE problem with the Hollywood model of being a boss is that it presumes that you, the boss, have awesome, omnipotent power, like one of those in the movies.

In reality it is extremely unusual for any manager to be an ultimate boss. You are more likely to be one of many managers in a lengthy chain of command. You sometimes see an omnipotent boss in tiny, private companies that are owned by just one person, like a corner shop or small PR agency. But most companies—and certainly all larger ones—are not structured like a corner shop.

In a moderately sized private company, the lowest level of manager might supervise a handful of employees. That manager in turn may have a boss in middle management. In larger companies there will be several layers of middle management before you arrive at the CEO.

While a CEO might want you to believe they are the ultimate boss, the truth is that the CEO will report upward again to a board of directors. Some of those directors will be the company's investors, typically from the venture capital sector. And those venture capitalists have bosses too—they are usually referred to as limited partners. Limited partners are investors who come from large financial institutions such as pension funds, insurance companies, or large financial foundations. Guess what? Limited partners also have bosses inside their own companies. And those companies have CEOs, and those CEOs have boards of directors.

Likewise, in publicly traded companies—those with shares that are sold on the stock markets—the setup has equivalent parallels: The directors will be in thrall to their larger investors, who will be coming at the company from all angles with demands for improvement.

That is what management is like in real life. The folks beneath you may regard you as a very powerful beast indeed. But you will know that the beasts above you are many times more fearsome.

The chain of command creates an unfortunate tendency for people to push their problems upward to the managers above them. The intent is innocent enough. No one wants to make a mistake. People want their decisions to be approved by their bosses. Managers want to know if there are problems at work, and staff may need their authority to get things done.

This generates the monkey on your back problem.

The problem is named after a 1974 article in *The Harvard Business Review*, which the journal says is "one of the publication's two best-selling reprints ever." In the article, William Oncken, Jr. and Donald L. Wass describe a manager with four staff members who keep asking their boss for help. Every time they encounter a problem, they ask their boss for a solution. But, Oncken and Wass note, every time a staff member asks their boss to solve a problem, it makes the monkey on their back jump to their boss: "Let us suppose that these same four subordinates are so thoughtful and considerate of their superior's time that they take pains to allow no more than three monkeys to leap from each of their backs to his in any one day. In a five-day week, the manager will have picked up 60 screaming monkeys—far too many to do anything about them individually."

The article describes the hapless manager's solution. He comes into work on Saturday morning to clear the backlog: "He returns bright and early the next day only to see, on the nearest green of the golf course across from his office window, a foursome. Guess who?"

HOW ARE YOU GOING TO SOLVE THIS PROBLEM FOR ME?

The solution is to give your staff the power to solve problems themselves, or at least to train them that if they come to you with a problem, one of your most frequent responses will be, "Tell me how you are going to solve this problem for me?"

The purpose is *not* to push all problems downward to the lowest level of workers. That would be asinine. It is to make sure all your employees are thinking two steps ahead, and to give them the power to fix things themselves. You don't want them to turn *their* problems into *your* problems when it would be quicker for them to just solve the problems first.

Nonetheless, to return to the manager with 60 screaming monkeys, you can see that pushing all those monkeys back down the chain again doesn't immediately solve all those problems. It merely transfers them to other staff who may or may not be able to fix them. You might create a situation in which your workers despair—there are now 60 monkeys running around the place and no guidance from management.

That is where prioritizing comes in. (We discussed the value of this in the chapter on increasing productivity.) Mostly, prioritizing is about ensuring that staff are working on the most important tasks all the time, with the ability to drop the least important ones.

But a crucial aspect is making sure your staff also have the right to ask you to set priorities. If your staff really do have 60 problems, it's a fair guess that they won't be able to solve them all in a week. They need to be able to come to you and say, "We cannot do all this. Which ones do you want done first, and are there any we can drop?" You need to be able to quickly clear their desks of the more trivial tasks.

Prioritize & delete, in other words.

WHY *MANAGING UP* IS INCREDIBLY IMPORTANT

While employees often feel comfortable bringing problems to their bosses and asking for solutions, the monkey problem has a mirror-opposite too: Employees often don't communicate upwards what is going well. Management often knows a lot less about what is going on at work than you'd think. This is counterintuitive. We do our jobs in front of our bosses. They can literally see what we are doing all day. How could this possibly be a problem?

But as soon as you get promoted into a managerial position, you will find that people tend to be reticent with their bosses, even when something is going well. They don't want to waste their manager's time. They don't want to show off. They don't want to look obsequious. They assume that if their boss wants something, they will ask for it. And if they don't ask for it, they must already have the information they need.

The result is that bosses can end up flying blind. Remember Dave, the guy who said, "I just want to know what the fuck is going on," even though he sat right next to his boss? That's how bad communication can be inside a company. People think that because they are in the same room, they are all on the same page. Not true.

Given that you are in a chain of command, you need to appreciate how information moves up and down that chain and why that is important.

It is usually easier to get information to move down the chain.

It is often more difficult to get good information coming back up. *Up* includes information coming up to you, and also you moving information upward to those above you. As a manager, you need to be able to champion, defend, and show the value of the work your team does in a meaningful way. The work they do reflects on you. And you need the chain of command above you to see that work.

Similarly, you need the staff below you to communicate what they are doing upward—with checkable data—for the exact same reason.

TWO WAYS OF MANAGING UP

Managing up thus involves communicating in two ways:

1. Telling the people above you what you are doing. You need to communicate to the chain of command above you the value of the work that you and your team have done.
2. Teaching the folks beneath you to communicate upward to you the results of what they are doing. This is often overlooked. One way to make yourself a better manager is to make sure that everyone below you is managing up to you as much as you are managing down to them.

Managing up—getting communication to move continuously in both directions—is an incredibly undervalued skill. Managing up isn't just about pushing problems upward or downward. Ideally, it is about seeing the business you are managing holistically, and making it easier for both your staff and your managers to run that business.

TEN-SECOND CHEAT SHEET

⌚ Most managers exist in a chain of command. They do not have omnipotent power.

⌚ You will need to manage up and down that chain.

⌚ You will be surprised at how difficult it can be to see what staff beneath you are doing without data.

⌚ Communicate upward, with data, the value of what you and your people are doing.

⌚ Teach your staff to manage up to you in the same way—with checkable data.

⌚ Don't let staff give you the monkey on their back.

⌚ Give staff the power to solve problems themselves.

⌚ Setting priorities will avoid gridlock.

⌚ Give staff the right to ask you to set priorities—so they are not trying to fix everything all at once. Your staff need to know they can ask you to prioritize their work.

17

Encouraging level-four behavior

So far, so good.

You are encouraging your staff to be reliable, low-drama, and highly productive. They are crankers and builders who get it right first time. They are managing up.

These are all qualities that make someone good at the job they currently have. When you are considering a promotion for a member of staff, you need to look for qualities that show they might be good in the future at the more senior role.

What does that look like? Here is an example:

A former colleague (whom I'll call Robyn) once told me a story about a nightmarish project she handled at Bloomberg. The company publishes an annual review of changes to international tax law. (I know. Tax law. Try not to get too excited.)

This review is a big, complicated project and it hinges on an annual tax deadline which, obviously, cannot be moved. The tax review covers 114 countries and requires finding a lawyer in each country to write a guide to all the changes in that country's tax regulations since last year. That guide then needs to be looked at by a series of legal, technical, and compliance editors. The guide is relied on by thousands of lawyers and tax accountants all over the planet, and it absolutely must be delivered on time.

Normally, the guide is simply updated each year. But this time around, Bloomberg's editors wanted to publish it in a new format—and no one realized that the new format tripled the amount of work required.

In Robyn's telling of the story, she began red-coding the sections of the guide that were going to fail to meet the deadline, and realized quickly that most of the guide was now in the red. There was no chance of delivering it on time.

Bloomberg customers pay tens of thousands of dollars annually for their subscriptions. Not delivering would be a colossal failure. This is also every journalist's personal nightmare: Realizing, to your horror, that there is absolutely no way to complete your project before a deadline that cannot be moved.

Her solution wasn't spectacular, but it worked. She went to her bosses, explained the situation, and persuaded them to allow her to hire more editors to get the job done. They also turned the package from a single product published at a single time into a two-part package, where one part was published by the original deadline and the other followed in the weeks afterward—thus allowing her team to get *something* out the door on time while they scrambled to get the rest of it done.

OK, so this tax review anecdote isn't the wildest story I have ever told! But it showed me that:

- Robyn realized ahead of time that the company was facing a big problem.
- She proposed a plan to solve it.
- The work eventually got done.

Robyn turned out to be one of the best managers I have ever worked with. That's because Robyn was exhibiting level-four behavior.

Put simply, an employee operating at level four is someone who has mastered their own job and also understands the job of the manager above them well enough to do that. A level four staffer is a very good candidate for a promotion.

I learned the idea of level four from my colleague John Heggestuen, the vice president for strategy at Insider Intelligence, the market research unit of Insider. Back in 2018 John wrote an advice column for people trying to get promoted. The article, published on Insider, divided employees into four types, according to how they solve problems at work.

John described this much better than I can, so I am going to borrow from his article heavily. (The original was titled 'Here's exactly what to say to show your boss that you're good at your job' and was published on November 15 2018, if you want to read it yourself.)

The four levels look like this:

Level one: I have a problem. What should I do?

"This is a very junior way to communicate a problem. You are creating more work for your manager because you are asking them to solve the problem for you," John says. This person is not ready to be promoted. (If you have staff who have been with the team a long time and they still operate like this, you might want to consider replacing them.)

Level two: I have a problem. Here are potential solutions.

A level two staffer is still presenting their manager with problems to be fixed. They are still creating work rather than solving problems. But now, at least, they are thinking the problem through to the solution. "Just showing that you've thought about how to solve a problem is an indicator of next-level potential," John says.

Level three: A problem came up. These were my options.
I chose to do this, and here's why. It's handled.

This type of employee clearly knows the business inside out, and wants to get the work done. They are keeping their manager in the loop. And, obviously, there is an element of trust, because this employee is reliable enough to solve problems without management's involvement. "'It's handled' is music to a busy manager's ears," John says, "and it doesn't create additional work."

Level four: It sounds like you are having this problem.
Here are some options to solve it.

This person isn't just taking care of business. They are anticipating problems that have not yet arisen and coming up with tactics to avoid them. They are predicting their manager's needs and devising ways of meeting them. "This is someone who is operating at the next level," John says.

TEN-SECOND CHEAT SHEET

⌚ When you are considering a promotion for a member of staff, you need to look for qualities that show they might be good in the future at the more senior role.

⌚ Look for level four employees—people who are anticipating and solving problems before they arrive.

⌚ Level one staffers are always asking you to solve their problems.

⌚ Level two staffers can identify solutions but still want you to decide the answers for them.

⌚ Level three people handle problems for you, and communicate that.

⌚ Level four people anticipate your problems in advance and suggest strategies before those problems arrive.

18

Use goal-setting to end management by anecdote

SEVERAL years ago, I was managing a team that had grown from just three members of staff to about 30 people in the space of a couple of years. Yet for the most part, I was still managing the office as if we were a small group, all sat at the same table, in earshot of each other, all operating on the same set of assumptions. The dinner party problem, in other words: I was acting like I was still the host of an intimate meal for four, when I should have been behaving like the conductor of an orchestra.

The time came for the annual performance review of one particular staffer: Let's call him George.

At a meeting with the six managers who helped me run the office, I asked them how George had performed over the year. Everyone agreed that they liked George. He was great. He will do anything you ask, they said. They told me several anecdotes about how much fun George was to work with.

"Fantastic," I said. "But what did he achieve over the last year, exactly?"

There were a lot of blank looks at the table.

It turned out that—through no fault of his own—George had been moved from one team to another. One of his managers had left the company and been replaced with a new one. His duties had changed. And the result was that George had fallen through the cracks: No one had been consistently tracking the work he had done.

I was livid. It was like being in a sitcom about bad management.

"OK," I said, "So you're telling me that *none* of you have been tracking his performance? We don't know whether he deserves a promotion or whether we should let him go?"

I told the team to do some detective work and come back with actual data showing me what George had been up to for the last year. The good news is that, after two weeks of digging, we were able to figure out that George had in fact been involved in several projects that were important for the company. He deserved credit for this. So we gave him a pay raise.

But you can see how unfair to George this whole situation was. His managers (including me) had failed him by not tracking, collating, or presenting performance data about his work on a monthly basis. Companies make hiring, firing, promotion and compensation decisions based on their ability to measure how well individuals perform, or to spot underperformance. Had we been less careful, it might have cost George his job. (We didn't tell George about any of this behind-the-scenes drama, of course!)

Crucially, tracking staff performance with objective data prevents management by anecdote, which is what we were doing with George. It was nice that George was great to work with and a popular colleague. But—as I have mentioned before—work isn't a popularity contest. It's a getting-things-done contest.

As a manager, your decisions are incredibly important to your staff—financially and for the progression of their careers. Your decisions need to be accurate, and that means looking broadly at everything they have done since their last review. Not just the most recent stuff. Not just the stuff that stuck in your head. Not based on anecdotes or impressions.

Usually, checkable data will be your best friend. Whatever

your staff are responsible for, turn it into numbers that can be tracked over the long term. Did the staff member hit their goals or not? Did they overperform or underperform? Should they be promoted or not? Numbers can describe this. Not just their performance over the last couple of weeks but over the long term—12 months or more.

GOALS THAT WORK

Of course, humans aren't robots. Quality matters too. You should use performance review meetings to set goals for your staff that encourage creativity, ambition, responsibility for new projects, or the development of new lines of business. Some of these will not easily be measured on a spreadsheet. Some of them *should not* be measured on a spreadsheet. You should give staff a chance to shine in terms of both quantity and quality.

I recommend staff be given three major goals to hit every quarter:

- A quantitative goal (something objectively measurable with numbers).
- A qualitative goal (something about increasing the ambition, sophistication, or scale of their work).
- And a *wild card*, or customized goal, based on the staffer's individual circumstances.

These goals should be shared in writing with each staff member, so that everyone can see what the staffer achieved in the previous quarter and everyone knows what they are aiming for in the next one. Quarterly performance reviews are good because they require managers to examine, and give credit for, staff successes. Managers don't always see all the good work people do, as I learned with George. They also help managers see where staff are falling down and intervention may be required. Or maybe the goals were impossible to meet, and the manager needs to think again.

And by the way, goals should actually be *goals*—achievements that are challenging but realistic. Goals should not be mere descriptions of the basic activities required by the person's job. Put another way, if you are setting goals that say things like, "Arrive at work on time in the morning," then you are going wrong.

The last portion of the review should be open-ended so that staff can ask questions about the company, what the bigger plan is, and where they fit into the greater scheme of things. This is especially useful if staff don't get a lot of one-on-one time with you. People aren't psychic. They don't know what you are thinking, how you see things, what you regard as good or bad in the business. Unfortunately, precisely because they are not psychic, they often guess at what is going on—and their guesses can be wildly wrong. (This is another good reason not to practice mushroom farming.) You want everyone to be on the same page and quarterly reviews are a useful tool for achieving that.

TEN-SECOND CHEAT SHEET

- Each manager should schedule a formal performance review with all the staff who report directly to them, individually, once per quarter.

- Performance reviews should look at whether the employee hit both quantitative goals (as measured by numbers) and qualitative goals (as measured by judgment).

- The review should take a long view, looking back over at least the last nine months of their work so you can observe long-term performance.

- Performance reviews should include good data. Avoid management by anecdote.

- Be direct and transparent when you discuss an employee's progress. Good employees want praise and credit for things they did well but also guidance and help when it comes to aspects of the job that went poorly.

- The performance review should be used to set goals for the next quarter, which should be written down. Make it clear what you actually expect to be done.

- Consider setting each team member three important goals per quarter. Fewer than three is probably too easy to hit in a three-month period. More than three feels overwhelming.

- If you want to encourage staff to manage up to you, ask them to write their own performance reviews of themselves before the meeting—that way you can see whether the staff member has a realistic idea of their progress.

19

Pay negotiations: *"What the hell does it take to give someone a pay rise in this town?"*

IN the spring of 2018, Bitcoin was (again) all the rage. The price of Bitcoin reached nearly $19,000, a dizzying height at the time. Investment money was pouring into various cryptocurrency businesses and their underlying blockchain technologies. Every time Insider published a story about Bitcoin, reader interest was intense. Our stories frequently went viral as Bitcoin investors—and clueless civilians looking to get rich quick—devoured every scrap of available information about crypto schemes.

Interest was especially fierce in London, the world's capital of fintech (financial technology companies). Venture capitalists had funneled hundreds of millions of dollars into a vast array of new technology startups that sought to disrupt traditional banking. You have probably heard of some of them: Foreign currency exchange companies like Transferwise (now called Wise), online banks like Revolut, peer-to-peer loan investment companies like Zopa, and debit card replacement apps such as GoCardless.

Yet Insider did not have a writer solely dedicated to covering cryptocurrency in London. We needed one.

So I persuaded a reporter at a rival company to have coffee with me purely because he was a specialist in cryptocurrency. Crypto is complicated stuff. The number of journalists who actually understand how cryptocurrencies work, and have a network good enough to keep them supplied with interesting new stories, is tiny. There were probably fewer than ten in London who knew what they were talking about at that time. Globally, there were no more than a dozen or two more.

We met at a trendy cafe in the lobby of the Leman Locke hotel in Aldgate, on the southern edge of Shoreditch in London. The Leman café has a bright, airy upper floor with windows on three sides looking down into the street below. It is decorated with Scandinavian-style polished wood and exposed metal railings. Potted plants hang over the bar.

The reporter I arranged to meet arrived before me. He was the epitome of Shoreditch hipster style: trendy glasses with thick frames, a small beard, and unruly hair swept back with gel. He wore a deliberately old-fashioned checked jacket. He had spent a long time making himself look slightly untidy.

We made smalltalk about the industry.

While I respected his knowledge of the business, he was also clearly enjoying the fact that he was in heavy demand from his own sources (who craved the good publicity that came with being mentioned in his articles) and the number of potential employers that wanted to hire him.

I eventually got around to the point. Would he be willing to come work for me?

"No," he said.

I went around the houses again, but he repeatedly made it clear that he was very happy at his current employer and was not looking to move.

Journalists are often paid very poorly. Many conclude from this that the wages they earn in their current job are similar to those being paid elsewhere. This is not the case. In reality, compensation in the media varies wildly. Some journalists at the top of their game—those with valuable expertise, exceptional networks, deep levels of sourcing, and many years' experience—can command handsome salaries. My coffee date—like many journalists—appeared not to know this.

I persisted. What would it take, I asked, to get him to move over to my company?

He wouldn't take the bait. "I am not looking to move right now," he said.

"But aren't you at least curious about what we could offer you?" I asked.

"No," he said.

I grew frustrated at his lack of interest at what was potentially on the table. So I took a gamble. "Tell me what your current salary is," I said. "I'll double it."

To be clear, I had no idea what he currently earned and did not know if I could make good on such a promise. I simply wanted to get his attention, to find out where his starting point was.

There was a pause. And then he shook his head. He didn't even throw out a number. He didn't ask what I might pay him. He simply insisted he wasn't looking to move.

I laughed, picked up the bill, and walked back to my office thinking, "What the hell does it take to give someone a pay rise in this town?"

I have interviewed hundreds of job candidates and been through hundreds more compensation negotiations. It is surprising how few people ask about money. You never know what kind of opportunity you are dealing with if you don't ask.

HOW TO NEGOTIATE COMPENSATION

Anyone who works, at some point in their lives, has to ask about pay and be prepared to negotiate. What follows is my advice for anyone—management or otherwise—who is involved in any kind of pay negotiation.

As a manager, you will probably be responsible for setting the pay rates of the people you supervise. And, of course, when you are promoted you will probably be offered a pay rise yourself. So it is worth learning how pay negotiation works in the real world, both for yourself and for your staff.

This chapter deals with pay negotiations, promotions and compensation—from both sides of the table.

WHAT A BAD NEGOTIATION LOOKS LIKE

It is very common for employees to come into an annual performance review and say something like this: "I deserve this. I have worked really hard. I have done everything that you asked me to do. I know other people in similar positions at the company make more money than me. I feel I deserve a raise."

This is a very weak case.

Working hard, doing your job, and following instructions are the minimum requirements for employment. They are not proof that your work is so productive that the value of it has increased. Lots of people make more than you. That's life. Your feelings aren't worth money.

WHAT A STRONG CASE LOOKS LIKE

A strong case is when you can demonstrate clearly—with facts and data—that you are very productive, that your work is of a visibly higher standard than your peers', and that keeping you around is a good investment.

The key is facts and data. It is very difficult to say *no* to managers or staff with a clear track record of superior performance, demonstrated with data.

SO HOW DO YOU GET THERE?

Negotiating compensation starts before you have even started the job, and before you get your next job. So the first order of business is...

Take the call

I have spent a lot of my time recruiting. For just one executive-level vacancy, I screened or interviewed more than 90 people. Many of them were folks I was trying to poach from competing companies. We advertised the position publicly, of course. But at the same time, I was messaging, emailing, and sending notes to a dozen or more specific individuals whose work I admired at other brands.

The most surprising thing about trying to poach rival talent is how few people even bother to respond to a request for a conversation.

If you don't have a conversation with someone trying to recruit you, you won't know what is on offer or how much money they might be willing to pay you. It doesn't matter if you don't want the job. That's not the point. Taking the call helps you find out how much you are worth elsewhere. (And, if you are the recruiter, it helps you figure out how much rival talent is being paid.)

Ask how much they are willing to pay

Do your research. Network. Talk to friends or colleagues at competitors about what it is like elsewhere. Ask how much you could expect to make. It's market research.

Do not tell a job interviewer what you currently make

This is a classic negotiation mistake. The employer usually has no idea how much you are currently paid. Even in management, you will be operating with substantially less information about compensation than you would like. Most managers have no idea how much their peers make, or their bosses. And they have only anecdotal information about what comparable staff at rival companies make.

In any given compensation negotiation, both parties are usually working with incomplete knowledge about market rates of pay. So blurting out what you currently make only helps them—by adding to *their* knowledge but not adding to *yours*.

Companies do know how much one of their own workers or managers is worth. If you say "I earn $70,000," and that number is less than what they currently pay others, then that employer will probably offer you a little bit more than $70,000 as a pay rise. Congratulations! You have won yourself a small raise! But you might become annoyed when you find out that your employer generally pays $90,000 to similar staff.

Telling potential future employers what you currently earn also solidifies legacy pay disparities, especially for female, Black, Asian and minority workers, because a lot of companies simply base your new pay on whatever you told them your old pay was. So ask for what you want, not what you currently have.

To avoid this trap, do two things:

1. Maintain current knowledge of what the market pays for workers and managers like yourself. Take the call, even if you don't want the job. Ask your friends in the business what they earn. Do research on the internet. Have some idea of what you could be making.
2. Tell recruiters—or your bosses—what you *need* to make. Do not relate this number to your current pay. Dream big!

The worst that can happen is they will say *no*.

Most importantly, don't be afraid to negotiate. Compensation is strictly business. The time to negotiate is when you are being recruited for the job and when you are in a formal performance review. It is smart to attempt to obtain the full value of your work from an employer. Good companies will not mark you down for trying to maximize your value. (And if they do, then in reality you are not working for a good company and you need to update your LinkedIn profile and move elsewhere.)

Of course, there are stumbling blocks.

Realize that different companies will pay different rates

The BBC pays much less than competitors because it is a prestigious place to work. Bloomberg pays much more than rivals because it has a lucrative business model—highly priced subscriptions for special computer terminals filled with market data—that other companies don't. Similarly, Apple, the most influential technology company on the planet, generally pays a little less than other technology companies simply because so many other people want to work for Apple. (Conversely, there are older, and less cool, tech companies that offer handsome compensation precisely because everyone else wants to work at Apple.)

So you may not always be able to name your price. The price may change depending on the company you are dealing with.

Begin your pay negotiation a year ahead of time

Once in the job, you want to be able to demonstrate across a full year that your work has superior value. Don't approach a pay review on a last-minute basis, citing things you did recently. Play the long game.

Demonstrate your value with data

Track your own data. What does your company value? In digital media, managers often look closely at the number of readers each writer or editor attracts. In sales, you may be judged by the total amount of revenue you generate, or the number of units you sell regardless of price, or the number of new clients you brought in, or even something as workaday as the number of phone calls you make.

Whatever that metric is, track it yourself. Don't rely on your boss to track your performance for you. And by *track* I mean literally create a spreadsheet in which you record this information on a daily, weekly, or monthly basis.

This will help you ensure that you increase your success over time. And it will help you figure out if you are doing better or worse than your colleagues. You'd be surprised how few people track their own data themselves. They often rely on their companies to do it for them. That's fine, but your best advocate is you. So track that performance data yourself.

Be above average... and prove it with data

You'd be surprised by the things management is not seeing. Find out what an average staff member gets in terms of user traffic or subscriptions or sales or contracts. Once you know that, make sure your results are above the average of your colleagues.

Demonstrate your growth

Your company may set goals for you, but in the long run it doesn't really matter what those goals are; the most important thing is whether you are consistently improving your performance over time. That is because companies tend to invest in growth generally, not in you as an individual, and not in a specific target. Use the whales & fails process to improve your stats by a little bit each month. Those gains will compound on each other and make you look good over the course of a year.

And, because you are tracking this data yourself, you will be able to show this proof in a chart when you negotiate your compensation.

Find out what your boss needs to deliver, and deliver it

Your goals should be based in large part on your boss's goals. So find out what they are, and deliver them. It's not rocket science. Making your boss look good will help ensure that your boss will want to pay you to stick around. This is level four behavior, which we discussed earlier in the book.

Take on new initiatives

Just doing the basics of your job is fine, but it's easier to make a case if you have gone above the call of duty. Perhaps you have led a new project, or developed a new product. Be ambitious. Good managers value employees who are highly flexible and comfortable with change. Leading something new is a way of showing that.

Low drama, high productivity

I talked previously about how I prize staff who are low on drama and highly productive. Doing a great job with a minimum amount of fuss or controversy is incredibly valuable. Just knowing that I don't have to worry about something you are in charge of has its own value.

"I have always just accepted the pay rises I have been given"

It is a cliché that people who say this often believe they are paid less because they don't aggressively negotiate their pay rises. It is equally a cliché that those who negotiate like demons end up with more.

Neither is consistently true.

While I definitely think you should learn about market rates of pay and be prepared to negotiate, simply saying *yes* to pay rises when they happen is actually *not* a terrible career strategy. The gains compound over time. Remember, a 5% raise this year is also a 5% raise next year (over your previous salary). The gain recurs annually, not just once.

More is more. Appreciate it.

How much management bandwidth are you sucking up?

Now let's talk about the bad stuff. Look at your boss and count how many people they supervise, in total. Then divide the number of working hours in a week by the number of people they supervise. That tells you, on average, how much time they have available each week to deal with you. A manager supervising a team of five can only devote one-fifth of her attention to you. That's less than two hours per day. (An eight-hour day divided by five equals 1.6 hours.) So if you are taking up more of her time than that, it had better be for high-value reasons. If you are taking up excessive amounts of her time with nonproductive problems… eh, good luck with that. You are going to mark yourself out as a pain in the ass.

The company may simply be unable or unwilling to pay you what you want

You may be asking for way too much. The company might simply not have the budget for it. The company's business model may be changing, making your work less valuable. Remember, the company is not even required to keep you employed.

Be aware of your leverage

Workers only have one type of leverage—the implied threat of leaving. Your threat leverage is therefore essentially weak unless you are something like a Hollywood star or a TV news anchor, where the entire enterprise depends on your specific face and charisma.

Even in highly personal jobs—such as sales—where relationships are everything, very few companies ever collapse because one key person leaves. Leaving is usually not much of a threat. So you're going to need a more positive case. Use sugar, not vinegar.

Assess how difficult it would be to replace you

If you control a key relationship with a client or an important connection with a set of valuable sources, or have simply succeeded at a task where previously there was failure and chaos, it might be difficult to replace you—and that improves your compensation case. Employers often try to imagine how troublesome it would be if you left. If *only you* can do what you do, you might have a strong case. But if you are doing a job that hundreds of others could do, you need to realize that "I quit" is not your strong point.

Remember, the vast majority of people falsely believe that they are difficult to replace.

Consider whether the company would benefit if you left

Few people think about this.

But sometimes management is pretty happy to see you leave. It saves the company money. It opens up a desk for fresh blood. Maybe that money can be better spent on someone else. Veiled threats to depart might be less threatening than you think. Plus, they mark you out as someone who isn't committed.

Go get a job with another company

Sometimes you can end up in a rut, or your company simply undervalues what you do because you have been in the same role a long time. It is usually valuable to get a variety of experiences on your résumé. And a new job usually means more money (After all, why else would you take it?)

Boomerang back later

If you leave a good company on good terms, it is possible that after a year or more the company might want you back—and that is a great time to ask for more money. Good companies welcome back boomerang employees because although they may now be more expensive, their wider experience makes them more productive.

In the media business, there was only one company that, infamously, did not do this: The news service Bloomberg once had a policy that made it clear to staff that if they left, they could never come back. Bloomberg also generally pays its staff more than competing companies, in hopes of generating a level of financial anxiety that makes it very difficult for them to quit. This has been an effective strategy for retaining employees. If you have ever tried to recruit a Bloomberg employee, you will know how hard it is to get them to leave. They fear that once they resign, there is no possibility of going back, and this feels like a huge personal and financial risk.

However, this also puts Bloomberg at an interesting disadvantage. It cuts the company off from the massive pool of talent which consists of former Bloomberg workers who also have experience elsewhere. Those people, by definition, end up working at Bloomberg's competitors.

Specialize in something difficult

Staff who have very specific and rare experience can demand more money—especially if they have several years of that experience. That is not easily replicated.

When I was a pharmaceuticals reporter in the mid-2000s it became obvious that there were only six drug reporters on the planet who were worth reading. They could name their price. Do you have unusual skills? Or are there a lot of other managers who can do what you do?

Own your failures

I don't expect staff to succeed at everything all the time. That's not possible. People make mistakes. From management's point of view, it is easiest to organize our work if we get an early warning that something is failing. If you tried something and just weren't very good at it, be honest about that. Own it. Good managers need transparency. The ability to be honest, quickly, when you have screwed up is valuable. It makes you more trustworthy and reliable.

Don't be an asshole

You and your colleagues have to work alongside each other every day. Being an ass will ultimately count against you.

Don't be a malingerer

If problems at work are always someone else's fault, if you find yourself dissembling when things go wrong, or if you just can't see something from the other point of view (particularly your manager's point of view), then you are hurting your case.

Not every year is your best year.

TEN-SECOND CHEAT SHEET

- Think long term.
- Have a realistic idea of your market value.
- Go beyond your job description.
- Demonstrate growth, with data.
- Be above average.
- Do something difficult, repeatedly, and for a long time.
- Be low drama.
- When you screw up, own it.
- Successful people make it a habit of saying *yes* when they are being offered more money.

20

Toxic rock stars and knaves: The people you don't want on your team

O N only one occasion in my career have I ever heard of someone losing their job for outright refusing to do a task they were literally employed to do. This story was told to me by my friend Theresa, who worked at a news service in Brussels some years ago.

It was on a Friday, and this staffer—let's call him Mark—just point-blank declined to write a news story. Mark and Theresa worked on a team where their job was to cover the international investment banks in London, Paris, and Frankfurt. The big controversy that day was about the emergence of a link between Russia's President Putin and a European banking scandal. Putin, in addition to being the autocratic leader of a nation that is hostile to its neighbors in Europe and the West, is also reputedly the world's richest man. He and his allies among Russia's oil, gas, and manufacturing oligarchy have systematically milked those industries for personal cash. So the notion that some of Putin's money was being squirreled away in European banks—whose reputations are supposed to be squeaky clean—was tantalizing.

Mark, who had six months' experience, felt the story wasn't news, because Putin's family denied it. Theresa, who had 15 years' experience, felt the opposite: The allegation had been made publicly, it was rare for Putin's family to respond publicly, and everybody in the industry was talking about the investigation.

Mark just *would not* write the story.

After about 90 minutes of discussion, it became obvious that Mark believed the task was optional.

His refusal forced an issue.

This was no longer a debate about whether a story was newsworthy enough to be published. It was now about whether he was required, as an employee, to follow Theresa's instructions. Unfortunately, following instructions is an existential issue for a manager. Employment isn't a *choose your own adventure* activity. The work needs to be done. At a base level, it means doing what you are told. Given that, Theresa asked Mark to think about whether he wanted to return to work on Monday or not.

He did not return.

DO NOT THREATEN TO FIRE PEOPLE

In general, threatening to fire people if they don't do as they are told is a very bad strategy for a manager.

It is another one of those tropes from TV. *The Apprentice*— with its notion that workers ought to be fired on a weekly basis— has done a lot of damage. This is not how managing works in real life. If you have to threaten to fire someone, it means you have already lost control. It means the situation is unrescuable. It raises a question about you, the manager. How did you let it slide so far that firing someone now looks like the best solution?

Ruling through fear also works against you over time. Fear is not productive as a motivator. You want people to be enthusiastic about their work, not terrified of it.

THE DRUNK AT THE NEXT DESK

Nonetheless, sometimes you will encounter a colleague who is so recalcitrant or incompetent that they force the issue. My friend Tony once worked at a magazine whose editor-in-chief believed her staff should be treated as if they were part of a corporate "family." She wanted the company to look after its staff. She especially hated firing people, and almost never did. As a lowly writer, Tony liked this a lot. Knowing that it was extremely unlikely he would be fired was a comfort. It was nice to have job security. So, at first, Tony was supportive of this surrogate office family and its benevolent matriarch.

Time passed.

One Friday afternoon, Tony and a senior editor were working late, struggling to close the book (which is the industry lingo that means signing-off on error-free pages to be sent to the printer that night). Tony noticed that Mandy, the woman who worked at the desk next to his, was nowhere to be seen. She was meeting a source, the senior editor told him.

Next week, same thing. Tony's colleague was AWOL again. He toiled to finish the magazine without her help.

Tony realized Mandy was absent from the office quite a lot. She was always "meeting a source." And yet, the scoops she got from these sources were few and far between. She just wasn't writing very many stories.

"You don't get it—she's not meeting a source," the senior editor told Tony. He raised his thumb to his lips and tilted his head backward, miming someone drinking from a bottle. "She's meeting *the sauce*."

Suddenly Mandy's behavior made a whole lot of sense. She wasn't at work because she was drinking all the time. Technically, she did some work. She wrote a few stories. She did the bare minimum. She managed her job around her drinking schedule.

And here was Tony, grinding away like an idiot to get the magazine out the door. Doing extra work to make up for Mandy's lack of work.

This kind of unfairness is toxic. People aren't stupid. They can tell instantly when one of their colleagues is slacking off, and when they are being asked to do more than others.

Instead of ignoring the problem, Mandy's boss should have gently urged her to get help or treatment. They missed a potential happy ending, too. Perhaps Mandy could have returned to the office with her health restored. But they just let the situation drag on, which was bad for everyone.

So you can see there is a cost to not firing poor performers. Poor performers are unfairly taxing the rest of your crew with extra work. They are triggering resentment among your team. They are hurting morale.

FIRING PEOPLE IS THE WORST PART OF BEING A MANAGER, BUT SOMETIMES YOU HAVE TO DO IT

People are very afraid of being fired—for obvious reasons. But sometimes it is good to be fired, too.

At first glance, the idea that being fired is good for you sounds like the kind of absurd bullshit that only the most swivel-eyed Ayn Rand fan would spout. Yet it's true. There is no point in staying in a job you are bad at. Why would you want that? You can't build a career by doggedly sticking with an occupation where, every day, you know you are failing, your colleagues know you are failing, and your boss can see you failing.

I have been fired twice in my career. On neither occasion did it feel like the best thing that ever happened to me, as the cliché goes. But it definitely got me out of situations where I was going nowhere and achieving little. While I am not going to thank the people who fired me, I certainly don't regret being forced into something new.

So, while firing someone is generally an awful experience for the staffer, bear in mind that being fired doesn't last forever. It is temporary. It's just the first (forced) step toward them finding a new job where they will be more successful.

YOU ABSOLUTELY *SHOULD NOT* APPROACH FIRING PEOPLE IN A RANDOM, HAPHAZARD WAY

You need a clear understanding of why, as a manager, you need to fire someone. Getting rid of an employee is a serious issue. It will have a steep financial and emotional cost for the worker involved. So you need to know what you're doing, why you are doing it, and that the reason for your action is right.

This is crucial because, usually, it is not immediately obvious when one of your colleagues needs to be cut loose. More often, you begin to notice an accretion of small things happening over time. They start showing up late, repeatedly. They make mistakes, often. They say one thing, but do another. Other workers are avoiding them or complaining about them.

Each individual instance isn't a big deal. We all occasionally arrive late to work. But this person is popping onto your radar—in a negative way—with increasing frequency. The situation is compounded by the fact that the employee's performance is gradually getting worse. Maybe this person can turn things around. Maybe this person is just going through a bad patch. The only thing you will be sure of is that this is not a clear-cut decision.

Again, if their performance were outright terrible, it would be easy. But you'll learn that dramatically awful employees are the exception, not the rule. So you need a solid logic for dealing with poor performers who, for one reason or another, just aren't working out.

HERE'S A CHECKLIST OF ISSUES YOU SHOULD WATCH FOR

If any staffer ticks one or more of these boxes, you might need to think seriously about letting them go.

- **Is this person on board with the mission?** At a fundamental level, you need staff who agree with what the company is doing and who are working toward the same goal. If you have an employee who opposes the goals of the company, then why are you paying them?
- **Are they creating more work than they are solving?** A good proxy signal for whether someone is literally creating more work than they solve is to start counting the time you are spending in meetings discussing that person's performance. Your time is precious. It ought to be invested in your company's most important and successful activities. But if you are continually stuck in HR meetings discussing turnaround plans for one difficult staffer, then maybe this staffer is costing you more than they are helping.
- **People who are not succeeding.** Think back to the story I told you about the time I was a truck driver, routinely crashing the rig and spilling my cargo all over the loading dock. I was only able to do that job because several of my more competent colleagues cleaned up my messes as I went along. You do not want a person like this in your workplace. If a staffer cannot routinely execute the basics of the job then they have no business working for you.
- **High-drama people.** Who is generating the most drama in the office? Sometimes, very productive people are so enthusiastic about their work that they like to talk a lot about it, and generate office debates about what is going on. This is good—it is nice to have a buzz inside the office. But

sometimes you'll notice that one of your workers always seems to have a controversy or a crisis. Some people just love being the center of a drama. You'll also notice that, increasingly, people are pulling you into meetings to discuss what to do about this employee's latest drama. That's another red flag: The more of your time a single staffer takes up, the more you should ask yourself whether this person is a problem.

- **Knaves.** The former Google CEO Eric Schmidt had a practice of weeding out people who leak, lie, cheat or steal. He called it "maintaining low knave density." Too many knaves in the office hurts performance overall.
- **Toxic rock stars.** There is a workplace myth that you should tolerate rock star employees even if they are awful people because the results they get are fantastic. Wrong. People spend more time at work than they do with their families and friends, so it's crucial that folks at work are nice to each other. Collegial. Polite. That kind of thing.

Whenever you encounter a toxic rock star, ask yourself how productive and successful they are. If they are good at what they do, it may be worth tolerating their drama to keep them. But often it is simply the case that more drama equals more problems, and you might be better off without them.

If someone at work is grinding your gears, they're doing it to your colleagues too—and eventually that's going to affect the morale of the office. It doesn't matter how good they are. In the long run, they're going to poison the whole place.

What typically happens is that a rock star employee is genuinely getting great results for the company. But gradually, somehow, the rock star decides that the rules don't apply to them. They start skipping meetings because they feel they have better things to do. They show up late to work. They decline to be involved in the grunt work that is required of everyone else. Your other staff begin to notice that it's one rule for them and another for everyone else.

Slowly, the toxic rock star demonstrates to your staff that their workplace is unfair. In fact, *you* are being unfair: You let them get away with it. You are playing favorites. You are tolerating bullshit. Morale is sinking. But no one wants to say it out loud because the toxic rock star is still top of the charts when it comes to results.

Now you are in danger of losing the confidence of a majority of your staff who are doing most of the work.

It is a false economy to keep the toxic rock star because of their results. The damage they are causing is greater than their success.

TEN-SECOND CHEAT SHEET

- Firing people is the worst part of the job but sometimes you have to do it.

- Keeping a bad worker around harms the morale of the rest of the team. That worker is blocking a desk that could be used by someone who is awesome.

- Do not approach ending someone's employment in a random, haphazard way.

- If a staffer has any of the following issues, you might need to fire them:

  → They are not on board with the mission or seem to fundamentally resent working at your company.

  → They simply refuse to follow instructions.

  → They generate more work than they solve.

  → They are persistently unsuccessful at the work you need them to do.

  → They operate in a state of high drama.

  → They are a toxic rock star.

  → They are prone to lie, cheat or steal.

21

How to fire someone without being a jerk about it

O<small>K</small>, so you have an employee who is failing, or disruptive, or otherwise not doing the job they've been hired to do. Now it is time to intervene.

Firing someone should not be sudden. It should not happen on the spur of the moment, in a flash of temper. This isn't the movies and you do not want to create a scene.

The law in the US is usually quite lenient: you can fire someone "at will," as the law says, for any reason, at any time, as long as you are not discriminating against them. In practice, however, American employers do not randomly fire people at will, or on the spur of the moment. They generally use a deliberative process among managers before an employee is let go.

In the UK there are specific laws that govern when a person can be fired, and I will not summarize them all here. The key thing to remember is that the law is constructed around the concept of *fairness*. You demonstrate fairness by showing that there is a real reason you are letting the worker go, and that you treated them fairly on the way out. A real reason might include things like the staffer failing to turn up to work or failing to perform basic tasks. Firing someone should come at the end of a process that is fair and deliberative. And, obviously, you cannot fire people based on any kind of illegal discrimination hinging on their race, gender, religion, disability, age, sexuality or other protected characteristics.

When it comes to firing people, practice in the UK and US is largely similar. The desired result is that the firing should come as no surprise to anyone, including the employee being fired. Here is a good model to use, based on procedures I have seen at several different companies:

NO SURPRISES

First, give the employee a warning. Ask the staff member to attend a meeting about their work. When you request the meeting, keep the tone neutral. Don't say, "Can we discuss your shitty performance on the Smith account?" That just sounds like an ambush. Instead say, "Can we discuss the Smith account on Tuesday at 2 pm?"

Prepare for that meeting by writing the list of points you want to get across to the staffer on a sheet of paper. (You'll be surprised by what you forget to communicate once a meeting starts.)

In the meeting, start by asking the employee what they thought went wrong. It's best to hear their side first so that you are sure there aren't issues you have overlooked. You do not want any surprises.

After that, work your way down the list of points you prepared earlier, for example:

- You showed up late to the meeting with the Smith Co. client, and that is unacceptable.
- Your presentation to the Smith executives contained costing errors and spelling mistakes.

- You engaged the Smith executives in a pointless political argument at an after-work dinner, alienating the client.
- This behavior is below the minimum standard acceptable at this company. If there are further issues with your work performance, we will consider letting you go.

If you believe the employee can be rescued, you should also present them with a set of turnaround goals to hit over a given time period, so that they can prove they are able to continue working for you. Maybe you believe this employee is a diamond in the rough, making rookie mistakes. Perhaps they are new and inexperienced, and their errors are innocent. This is an opportunity for you, the manager, to use the warning meeting as a way to challenge, encourage and inspire them to do better. You might be surprised: Some people don't realize they are capable of doing better until they hear someone else say it to their face.

Then, after the meeting, send the employee an email summarizing what you just said. Keep the tone neutral and factual. Assume the worst-case scenario: Hostile employment lawyers may eventually see this email. You want that email to look like good evidence of your reasonable decision, not an example of your psychotic tyranny.

The employee has now been warned in writing. The ball is in their court. They can either get their shit together and rescue the job, or they can read the writing on the wall and get out.

If, at the end of the time period, they are still failing, then you probably have to let them go.

TEN-SECOND CHEAT SHEET

⊘ Firing an employee should come as no surprise to anyone, including the employee being fired.

⊘ If you fire someone, the decision should be fair and based on the real and demonstrable failings of the employee.

⊘ You need to be able to demonstrate that your decision to fire someone was fair and deliberative. For that, you need a plan.

⊘ First, give the staffer a written warning that describes what they did wrong, and what the minimum expectations for the job are. Give them a time period to turn the situation around.

⊘ If the staffer is still failing by the end of the deadline you set in writing, you probably need to let them go.

22

Problem solving:
How to prevent civil war
in your office

A LONG time ago I worked at a magazine with two editors who hated each other. It wasn't clear why they disliked each other, but they had always done so. The origin of their bad blood was lost in the mists of time. All anyone knew was that the guerrilla warfare had lasted years.

This conflict culminated when the female editor, whom I will call Andrea, contrived to have her rival Stephen fired after she obtained some juicy gossip about him, which she then weaponized. (I have changed the names and some of the details of this story for reasons that will become obvious.)

The building we all worked in had an old-fashioned design. Many editors had closed-door offices, like something from the TV show *Mad Men*. The problem with a closed-door office is that once the door is closed, no one knows what you are doing in there. It's great for the executive inside—finally, some privacy in which to work in peace! But everyone else just ends up wondering what on earth is going on behind that door.

So Andrea cooked up a plan.

She began to work late, staying behind after everyone else had gone home. She cultivated a relationship with the cleaning staff, making an overt effort to thank them for vacuuming the carpets and emptying the bins. Sometimes she would give them little gifts—bottles of wine, flowers, and fancy chocolates that had been sent to the magazine from grateful clients and sources. It did not take long before Andrea and the cleaning staff were on first-name terms, asking about each other's families, and bantering over whether the Mets or the Yankees had a better chance of winning a pennant that year.

After a few weeks of this subterfuge, Andrea triggered her plan. Noticing that Stephen had left for the day, Andrea flagged down one of her new janitor buddies. "Please can you help me, it's an emergency," she begged. "There's been a mixup. Stephen has left his office door locked for the evening and there's some work in there that I need to retrieve. It has to be done this evening! Could I borrow the key?"

Knowing that she was a longtime employee of the company and one of the magazine's top editors, they of course gave her the key. Then she sat down at Stephen's computer, switched it on, and fired up his internet browser. She looked at his internet history.

Surprise, surprise. Stephen had not been using his computer for work purposes during the day, to put it mildly. Andrea made a copy of the evidence she discovered, left Stephen's office, locked the door and returned the key as if nothing had happened. I don't know exactly what Andrea found on Stephen's computer, but it wasn't good. And I don't know whether Andrea confronted Stephen privately, or whether she handed the evidence to his bosses.

But the result was that Stephen left shortly afterward.

GRUDGES CAN POISON ENTIRE COMPANIES

This is absolutely *not* how to solve problems in the workplace. The failing here was that Andrea and Stephen's managers should have stepped in years earlier to reset the relationship and establish some professional ground rules. You can't have staff engaging in long-term espionage against each other.

In any workplace disputes that arise, people argue, and there will be conflicts about how to proceed. Left unaddressed, these conflicts can stagnate into internecine corporate grudges that can poison entire companies.

The most extreme example of a festering management dispute was possibly Enron, the Texas-based energy supplier that was once regarded as the US's most innovative company. At its peak in 2000, Enron's market cap was nearly $70bn. It collapsed amid scandal a year later.

One of the many, many reasons Enron went bankrupt was because its senior managers were engaged in an internal civil war with each other, undermining each others' businesses in an environment of secrecy and double-dealing. (There's a great book about this called *The Smartest Guys in the Room*, by Bethany McLean and Peter Elkind.)

Part of the collapse began with the pettiest of origins: Two of the most senior executives at Enron had an affair and then broke it off. They then adopted mutually opposing corporate strategies, from different wings of the company. This wasn't the sole reason for the end of Enron, of course. But it definitely didn't help.

My point is that leaving conflicts unaddressed is a very, very bad idea. If a workplace dispute occurs, you should work to resolve it as soon as possible. Don't ignore a conflict in the hope that it will disappear on its own. It won't.

TAKE YOUR ENEMIES TO LUNCH

Whenever I lock horns with a colleague, I know that the best thing to do is to take that person to lunch and smooth things over. Sometimes you have to eat lunch with someone you're fighting with.

Lunch is an interesting thing.

The act of sitting face to face, breaking bread, and observing table manners has a way of removing barriers between people even when those people regard themselves as enemies. There is something liberating about leaving the office and putting some nice food on the expense account. Most of the time, over lunch, when both sides have aired their views, the conflict suddenly feels a lot less important. And because lunch is an extended conversation, you're likely to end up with a much more nuanced idea of where the other person is coming from. Who knows, it might be you who is wrong! After coffee or dessert, compromise seems reasonable. No one wants to fight an endless war.

Lunch in a restaurant also gives the participants some privacy. It makes delivering bad news easier, or at least more dignified. It takes place away from the eyes of the office.

We have all seen a boss usher an underling into a conference room for a "chat." The long walk past the desks to the conference room door. The closing of the door for privacy. Perhaps the occasional sound of raised voices. And then, finally, the re-emergence of two unhappy people into the workplace.

It turns a simple disagreement into a needlessly mysterious public drama for the whole office. That's why lunch is superior to the conference room chat.

So, I say, take your enemies to lunch—and turn them back into friends.

LET THE REFUSENIK MAKE THEIR CASE IN PRIVATE

When you have a team member who disagrees with you, someone who is refusing to do the work that is asked of them, the last thing you should do is have a standup fight in the middle of the office in front of all your colleagues. It is tempting to raise your voice or get angry. I have done it. It does not end well. A screechy workplace meltdown always looks good on TV. But in real life, it is the one thing you are trying to avoid.

Instead, take a deep breath and control your temper. Remember, some workers have grown up in a digital environment where "trolling"—deliberately enraging your opponent with increasingly unreasonable statements—is considered normal discourse. Don't fall for it. (You're going to have lots of moments like this over the years, so the dramatic novelty of them wears off pretty quickly anyway.)

Take the refusenik into a private meeting and hear them out. A conflict will have a winner and a loser—and eventually you need the loser to agree to be on your side despite the blow to their ego. So lessen that blow by disagreeing with them only in private.

A good piece of advice here is to manage by asking questions. Don't assume that because you are the boss, you must be right and they must be wrong. There are more of them than you. They collectively know more about the job than you do. There is a pretty good chance that they know something you do not.

I sometimes take notes as they talk. That way, they can see that I am actively listening. And, if it turns out that I am dealing with someone who is determined to be disruptive, I have a record of the conversation.

Remain open to the idea that they might be right. If they *are* right, it is worth discovering that as soon as possible. This is also why you want to listen to them first. You need to make sure you have considered all the issues at stake. You are going to look like an idiot if you start by giving them a speech about why such-and-such needs to be done right now, only to learn as soon as your colleague replies that you've made a huge error—that they are right and you are wrong.

Figuring out that you are wrong, and changing course quickly, is a skill good managers need. Put your ego aside. It's just business.

MAKE THE CALL

Let's assume that after listening to their side, you still don't agree. Your instruction stands, and you want them to get on with the work you have assigned.

What do you say? I have a speech that goes a little something like this:

"I am happy to have the debate, and to hear your side. I have listened to you. But this is not a democracy. It's not college. You don't get to pick your courses. It is my job to make a call. On some days you are not going to like my decisions. That's OK. It is not possible or desirable for me to always make decisions that you agree with. We can't have everyone in the company doing whatever the hell they want. We need everyone to be on the same page. So you have to accept this decision now that it's made."

That usually does the trick.

NIP BAD THINGS IN THE BUD

Problems don't usually fix themselves. They usually slide and get worse. Bad bosses will often ignore a problem in the hope that it will go away. Nope. It will not.

Some years ago, a former colleague told me about an office he worked in where, after a while, he noticed that people were calling in sick a lot. The team started to become short-handed on a regular basis. What was going on?

The boss pulled all the staff's sick-day requests from the previous couple of months and dumped them into a spreadsheet.

He turned the data into a bar chart, broken down by the day of the week.

Normally you would expect illness to be randomly or relatively evenly distributed throughout the week. Not this time. Sick-outs on Mondays were triple the rate of sick-outs on Fridays. Clearly, some folks were calling in sick on Mondays to grant themselves a three-day weekend. Worse, newer staff were following the example of the veterans, and began concluding that Mondays were optional.

So the boss sent around a note reminding everyone that HR records their absences, that they can see a trend around Mondays, and that they expected a bit more than that. No one complained.

Monday stopped being a problem.

TEN-SECOND CHEAT SHEET

- Nip trouble in the bud: Problems don't go away on their own. You should step in quickly to resolve them.

- Left unchecked, petty personal disputes can wreck a company.

- Pull conflicts into a private discussion. Deliver negative feedback in private. Don't fight in public. A conflict will have a winner and a loser—you need the loser to agree to be on your side despite the blow to their ego. So lessen that blow by disagreeing with them only in private.

- You can soothe personal disputes by taking a colleague to lunch.

- Manage by asking questions.

- Accept that you might be wrong, and if you are wrong move quickly to reverse yourself. People respect those who admit they have made a mistake and rectify it quickly.

- Remember to listen and hear people out when they disagree.

- But equally, make it clear that it is your job to call the shots whether they like it or not.

- Try to track persistent problems with data so that you can measure how bad they really are.

- Don't have old-fashioned closed-door offices. They breed secrecy and laziness. Keep everything open-plan and transparent.

23

The dark arts: Tricks for dealing with difficult people

A LONG time ago, my friend Amelia told me this story about a writer she worked with who was on the take. Amelia was his editor at an online lifestyle magazine. One day a colleague came to her and said, "Have your staff started writing reviews of designer jackets?"

Amelia was baffled. "Of course not," she said. Her staff covered career advice and personal finance. They never wrote about clothes.

"Well that's weird, because one of your guys published a glowing review of a blue suede Christian Lacroix jacket on the website just before midnight," the colleague told her.

Amelia checked. She was right. For no reason whatsoever, one of her reporters had suddenly become an expert on jackets in the $500 price range, in the middle of the night.

"He came to me a couple of days ago and asked if he could review it, and I said *no*, because it looked sketchy," the colleague continued. "So when I saw this review go up anyway I figured you had said *yes*."

None of this made any sense.

Amelia decided to look into the mystery of the midnight jacket reviewer. When Amelia questioned the writer, it turned out that he had a friend at a PR agency representing the clothing brand. The unspoken—but obvious—agreement between them was that he could keep the fancy jacket if he wrote a review that was good for the designer.

It was a bribe, basically.

Amelia was incensed. This was a straightforward ethical violation. She decided to make him give the jacket back. "We might have screwed up by publishing a garbage review, but I was not going to let him profit from it by gaining a fancy jacket," she said.

The next day the writer told Amelia the company did not want the jacket returned because he had been wearing it for a couple of weeks. "Maybe I can just keep it?" he said.

He was trying to get away with it.

"No," Amelia said, "You're going to bring the jacket into the office and we are going to give it to charity. Maybe the Red Cross will take it."

After two more weeks of excuses—this guy was shameless, clearly hoping Amelia would forget—he brought the jacket into the office.

Amelia then began phoning various homeless charities to see if they wanted the jacket. To her surprise, she discovered that charities mostly do not want second-hand clothes. They are already inundated with them. This was becoming ridiculous. She couldn't even give the jacket away. So she ended up taking the jacket on her lunch break. She walked up Broadway until she saw a homeless person panhandling on the side of the street—a common sight in New York. "Would you like a new jacket? It's worth about $500, new," Amelia said, hoping he would realize that he might be able to sell it.

He took it, of course.

Somewhere in New York that week was a homeless man wearing an incredibly expensive jacket.

SAY THANK YOU FOR EVERYTHING

"NEVER INTERRUPT YOUR ENEMY WHEN
HE IS MAKING A MISTAKE"

Amelia should have fired the writer on the spot, but he was a new employee and—somewhat implausibly—he pleaded he had merely made a mistake. The magazine didn't fire people for mistakes, especially a first mistake, and Amelia couldn't prove his ill intent. So she settled for giving him a written warning instead.

Nonetheless, she now knew he was a liability.

Unfortunately, he was also a *successful* liability. The non-jacket stories he wrote did well with their readers. He earned a lot of traffic for the site. Letting him go would have hurt Amelia's results. He was a classic toxic rock star.

Time passed.

A month or two later, there came a day when Jacket Bribe Guy asked to meet Amelia for a private talk in a conference room. This was unusual. They sat down and he said he had received a job offer from another company. They were prepared to pay him more money and he was minded to take it. He was resigning. This made Amelia very happy.

"Congratulations!" she said. "It sounds like a great opportunity!"

"Wait," he said. "I was wondering if you'd consider making me a competing offer to stay?"

"I don't think I can, unfortunately," Amelia said. "I am very sorry to lose you."

Suddenly the writer looked worried. "The thing is, I haven't strictly said *yes* to the other guys yet..."

Amelia realized he had made a fatal error. He had resigned his current job *before* he had obtained a written agreement for the new one, in hopes of getting more money.

She was determined to make sure he left. "If they are paying you more money and you don't really want to work here, I can see why you are taking this new job. I accept your resignation." She walked out of the room.

Jacket Bribe Guy was leaving the building.

Napoleon once said: "Never interrupt your enemy when he is making a mistake." It is one of my favorite pieces of advice. You can benefit from it in almost any situation.

A FEW TRICKS FOR DEALING WITH DIFFICULT PEOPLE

I want to be clear about what I am *not* talking about. There is a certain type of manager who thinks that good management is all about the Hollywood model: scheming and plotting and backstabbing. This is absolutely not good management. Good management is about clear communication, encouraging talent, and solid organization (99% of the time). I am absolutely NOT advising you to run your team like Machiavelli. It might work in the movies, but not in real life.

However, you will frequently be asked to deal with difficult people. Customers, rivals, disgruntled employees. Every now and again the world throws some serious idiots at you. So it is worth learning a few of the dark arts to deal with them.

Listen first, act second

Listen more than you talk. This can be difficult for a manager, because you are expected to give out instructions all the time.

When some kind of conflict arises, you generally do not want to immediately weigh in with your opinion—you want to hear all the available evidence first. If you are dealing with someone who is slippery, you definitely don't want to assume anything.

This went through my mind when I was told the Jacket Bribe

Guy story. He made the mistake of thinking Amelia would want to keep him. Yet Amelia stayed silent until she could say the words, "I'll notify HR and we'll set a date for your last day in the office."

Don't start a fight unless you know that you will be the winner

Work is not the place for conflicts. It should not be a battleground. Being a source of constant drama is a good way to (eventually) get fired. You want to strive to make sure your teams are all on the same page—and you get that unanimity through good communication, listening, answering questions, discussing issues, and ultimately being very clear with your instructions.

If someone tries to engage you in a conflict, pause before rising to the bait. Ask yourself: Do you want to fight every single battle? Is every skirmish worth it? In the long run, the answer is usually *no*.

Having said that, disagreements arise and occasionally you might want to get your way. Pick your battles by having very few of them. Remember that there is no point in causing friction at work unless you have a very good chance that your side will carry the day. Don't start a fight unless you know before the fight starts that you will win. (To put it another way, if you know you're going to lose a fight, why bother?)

Keep your powder dry

Conflicts will cost you credibility, because every time you engage in one, your colleagues—or your bosses—will silently ask themselves, "How much longer do I want to deal with this?" On the flipside, if you engage in conflict rarely, your colleagues will be more interested in what you have to say; and perhaps more influenced by it, precisely because it is such an unusual event.

Everything you say or write can be used against you on social media

You might remember when the actor Tom Cruise lost his temper on the set of *Mission: Impossible* 7 in late 2020. He was trying to film the movie in the middle of the Covid-19 pandemic. An on-set rule was that everyone had to wear masks and maintain distance from each other to prevent Covid infections. He saw a couple of his staff casually chatting, close enough to infect each other. He blew up, and immediately entered Hollywood Bad Boss mode. A recording of him leaked to the tabloids. "I see you do it again, you're fucking gone!" he yelled at the crew. "I'm on the phone with every fucking studio at night, insurance companies, producers, and they're looking at us and using us to make their movies. We are creating thousands of jobs, you motherfuckers! I don't ever want to see it again. Ever!"

For a day or two, the world chuckled at Cruise losing his temper. Obviously, the management lesson here is: Don't scream "motherfuckers!" at your staff. They won't like it and they might make it public in an act of petty revenge.

From a management point of view, however, Cruise was absolutely right. A case of Covid among the crew could have shut down the whole production, possibly costing hundreds of thousands or maybe millions of dollars in lost time and extra expenses. Indeed, a few months later a number of *Mission: Impossible* workers did get sick, and filming was suspended for two weeks.

It didn't matter that Cruise was in the right. He used colorful language—and that caught everyone's attention. Had he shouted the same thing but without the F-bombs, few would have cared. Many more would have sympathized.

People no longer see a division between their private lives and their public lives online. If you do something mean or dumb at work, there is always a risk that one of your colleagues will turn it into a tweet, a Facebook post, or an Instagram video. People love to hate bad bosses and it takes very little to make a single bad moment go viral.

So, think before you speak. (And keep the cursing to a minimum.)

This rule applies even at small companies

One of the most-read stories we ever published at Insider was about the trendy cookware company Great Jones, founded by Sierra Tishgart. If you are the sort of person who wants your kitchen to look good on Instagram, then Great Jones was there for you. My colleague Anna Silman described the company like this:

"Great Jones' brand projected a vision of warmth and community. The company's colorful Dutch ovens and sleek stainless-steel frying pans had become a millennial staple in recent years, and Tishgart had fashioned herself into a prominent founder and influencer in her own right—wedding in *Vogue*, apartment in *Domino*, skincare regime on Into the Gloss. As everyone sought to relieve their pandemic anxiety by stress-baking sourdough and sharing photos of fluffy coffee and shallot pasta, the image that Tishgart and Great Jones sold had never been more appealing."

Behind the scenes, however, all was not well, Silman reported. Tishgart had made enemies among her own employees through a series of thoughtless actions. Great Jones was one of those companies where staffers left meetings in tears. When the mother of one of her employees died, Tishgart sent the staffer an email asking when she would be back at work *on the day of the memorial service*.

One day, five Great Jones employees and two former staffers wrote a 4,000-word letter to one of the company's board members, demanding that Tishgart be removed from the company. We see "no successful path forward where Sierra is in a CEO, leadership or people management position," it said. The letter leaked to Silman and, as they say, went viral. For a week it seemed like everyone on Twitter was talking about Great Jones and its problems, and the gap between its high-fashion image and the grim truth behind it. Even the venerable *New Yorker* magazine weighed in: "The saga suggests the gulf between the messaging and the reality of a certain type of online brand, and the ease with which customers accept the stories such companies sell."

It is important to remember that, at the time, this company employed only six people.

Six!

It did not matter that this company was tiny. The scale of the drama, not the scale of the operation, was the thing that caught the imagination of the internet.

Don't tweet

The above advice applies triply if you work for a large company. A long time ago, when Twitter was a tiny platform that only a small number of people had discovered, a man stepped off a plane in Memphis, Tennessee, and tweeted, "True confession but I'm in one of those towns where I scratch my head and say 'I would die if I had to live here!'"

The problem was that Memphis is the global air hub for FedEx, the international shipping company. And the man who got off the plane was a public relations executive who was making a presentation to FedEx executives that day. FedEx was one of his biggest clients.

They saw his tweet and were displeased. A bunch of FedEx employees wrote an email to their management, expressing their anger. "Many of my peers and I feel this is inappropriate. We do not know the total millions of dollars FedEx Corporation pays [your PR agency] annually for the valuable and important work your company does for us around the globe. We are confident, however, it is enough to expect a greater level of respect and awareness from someone in your position as a vice president at a major global player in your industry."

His tweet went viral, making headlines around the world. It was one of the earliest, most infamous "ill-considered tweets," as people used to call them. The FedEx staff noted archly in their letter of complaint: "A hazard of social networking is people will read what you write."

That's invaluable advice. *People will read what you write*. It doesn't matter that you thought only a few of your friends would see it. If you have written it down, the internet can use it against you.

The internet is a mean place, filled with bad-faith actors cynically feasting on the errors of people who are just trying to do their jobs without going bonkers. Memphis Man didn't mean to piss off an entire city and its major employer. He probably had a long flight, was tired and cranky, in need of a shower and some sleep, and had a stressful client presentation to complete. He thought that the only people reading his tweet were his friends.

As a manager, your actions and decisions will come under greater scrutiny than others. Everything you say and do and write is now public. You have no privacy at work.

You may also notice that the more senior an executive becomes, the more rarely they publish material on social media. The volume of a person's social media output usually exists in inverse proportion to their status at work. Now that you are a manager, you should seriously consider dialing back your social media output to a minimum.

HOW TO DEAL WITH LAWYERS

If you're in management, you're going to be dealing with your company's legal department.

The context here is that your company's lawyers are like all your other colleagues: They are good people trying to do their best. They are talented. They got through law school, which is not easy, after all! You should respect their wise counsel. It is absolutely true that 99% of the lawyers I have dealt with in my career have been consummate professionals. They have saved me from many mistakes. I owe them that. You want these guys on your side. You want them to make sure everything you do is straight-up legal. And you want them to threaten your awful, unethical enemies for their evil, illegal acts—which are continuous and legion!

However, here's the thing with lawyers: They are going to get in your way. There will come a day when you find yourself sitting in a conference room with a bunch of lawyers. You want to do something that is obviously common sense. And they will be telling you why common sense cannot possibly happen.

Why are these lawyers tormenting you so!

Lawyers tend to work from a single general principle: Reduce risk. This is baked into their genetic code. They can do no other. Reducing risk—and therefore expenses—for your company is what they do. Nine times out of ten, this is exactly what you need.

The problem with reducing risk is that there is one surefire solution that eliminates risk completely: Do nothing. And if your company always does nothing, it will go bankrupt in short order.

But there is a counterpoint to reducing risk, and that is defending the work. If you are in a position to choose your lawyers, then I highly advise instructing them that their mission should be to *defend the work*. You want to work with lawyers who help you get stuff done, not prevent stuff from happening.

Teach yourself some basic law

Many managers regard the law as an object of mystery to which they have no access, and act in abeyance to their lawyers at all times. They just do what their lawyers tell them to. The logical consequence is that your company will end up being run by your legal department—which negates the point of management completely. This is obviously problematic.

You cannot abdicate your judgment and outsource it entirely to your lawyers—especially if their desire to reduce risk ultimately requires your company to stop being in the business it is in.

So you should also educate yourself about the principal laws and cases that govern your industry. You should not kid yourself that you will end up knowing more than your lawyers—that is ridiculous. But you do need to know the right questions to ask, and the right legal strategies you need to get your work done.

Figure out what management above you will forget about

If you work in a busy, fast-paced environment, you will know what it feels like to receive multiple demands at the same time. It may be impossible to complete all the tasks your bosses want. You may also have experienced one of the most annoying aspects of modern working life: Being asked to do something, and then, once the project is completed, realising that your boss has forgotten that they wanted it done in the first place.

This happens to everyone. It will happen to you.

As a manager, you will repeatedly experience an underling happily report back to you that the project you requested is complete… while you silently draw a complete blank on what they are talking about. The way out of this is simply to say "thank you"—the two most useful words in the management lexicon. But also, take a mental note of the type of tasks that your managers forget about. Your job is to prioritize work for your team, by focusing on the most productive tasks and dropping those that drag the whole enterprise down, especially if your bosses have short memories.

EXERCISE YOUR POWER IN SILENCE

Two years after Jacket Bribe Guy resigned, Amelia received an email from him suggesting they might talk about whether he could come back to her company now that he had more experience. Clearly, he had learned that the grass was not greener at the other company and was trying to engineer his return. Amelia deleted his email without responding.

No need to make a fuss if you can dispatch a problem without being detected!

TEN-SECOND CHEAT SHEET

- Never interrupt your enemy when he is making a mistake.

- Listen first, act second. When some kind of conflict arises, you generally do not want to immediately weigh in with your opinion—you want to hear all the available evidence first.

- Keep your powder dry. Engage in conflicts as rarely as possible. Pick your battles by having very few of them.

- There is no point in causing friction at work unless there is a very good chance that your side will carry the day.

- Everything you say or write can be used against you on social media. So think before you speak or write.

- It does not take much to go viral for the worst reasons.

- Don't tweet.

- Small companies are not immune from excessive public scrutiny simply because they are small.

- Ask your lawyers to defend the work you do. Educate yourself about the principal laws and cases that govern your industry so that you can get the right decisions from them—and so that they do not end up being your bosses.

- Prioritize your team's work more efficiently by figuring out what other managers forget they asked for.

- If you can fix a problem without anyone else noticing—do it.

IV
—
DECISIONS

24

The worst job I ever had taught me the three most important things to know about management

THE first job I ever had was also the worst job I ever had. My boss, Bob (not his real name), owned the cardboard box factory here I worked as a packer and driver.

Bob taught me a lot about what really terrible ement looks like.

actory was located on a ridiculously grisly industrial edge of the Lake District in Northern England. The was unpaved. The parking lot consisted of dirt your vehicle in the shallowes

keep warm. (Cardboard needs to be kept *dry* but it
ed to be kept *warm*, I soon learned.)

ks carrying waste from nearby factories tipped their loads
the dock of our warehouse. Then six of us clawed through
e piles with our bare hands to rescue any discarded boxes that
were in good enough condition to be folded flat and used again.
The company—which I won't name because, remarkably, it is still
in business—then sold the recycled boxes back to the companies
that had paid us to take them away.

I spent my hours folding cardboard, placing it on pallets, then
tying those pallets down tightly with stiff plastic bands, so they
could be shipped out again as good as new. There were days where
we moved mountains—literal mountains of waste card—to turn
around more truckloads than we expected, clearing bottlenecks
in innumerable other companies' ability to ship packets around
the Northwest.

By the time I got home, I was covered in a thick film of
cardboard dust. It got everywhere: my hair, my eyebrows, m
mouth. When I blew my nose, the snot came out cardbo
brown. My clothes turned brown. My pillow cases became

The conditions were filthy, and so was the pay.

I received £3 per hour (somewhere around $4). S
coll gues had spent time in prison. People
e they were desperate, becaus
y was the box facto

mana

The

estate at the

road to the factory

and puddles. You had to park

you could find.

The main warehouse was made of cheap conc

corrugated iron. Inside was a maze of flattened cardboar

into towers two floors high, on wooden trucking

shuffled these cardboard towers around inside the wa

a battered forklift truck.

It was unheated, poorly lit, and partially open

The weather outside was the weather inside, esp

This was Northern England, so you had to w

rown.

ome of my

worked for Bob
they had no other alternatives. We just

at the Bex...

e money.

WHEN BAD IS AVERAGE

the factory's only executive. While the rest of us
...s, and overalls, Bob wore a tweed jacket, a red
and ancient corduroy trousers. Sometimes he

smoked a pipe. While we worked in the warehouse, Bob stayed in his office, making phone calls and keeping the books.

His style was aloof, cold. He couldn't understand why so few people wanted to work for him, or why his workers left so frequently. And he didn't bother to find out.

You might think Bob was uniquely bad. But in some ways Bob was merely average. A lot of managers run their businesses like this—they just do the job with as little thought as possible. As long as today's orders are filled, the job is done. Nor was this situation entirely Bob's fault. Bob inherited the factory from his father. It was all he knew. The factory had always been there, and always would be. And to give Bob credit, the factory did indeed stay in business, day after day, year after year.

But under no other definition could life at the factory be described as *good*. Every day was the same as the last. We, the workers, came to work, stacked boxes until 5 p.m., and then left. We never took on new projects, developed new lines of business, or did anything special.

That's because Bob had no plan. Bob had no strategy for where his factory might be in a month from now, a quarter from now, or a year from now. At no point were we ever told what the vision was. We didn't even know who our competitors were. Did other companies in the area offer higher-quality boxes? Were they cheaper? Did they deliver faster? Bob never talked about them and we never met them. The factory was stuck, drifting, marooned on an empty sea where nothing changed.

And of course, Bob never said "thank you." That was my first, easy lesson from the box factory.

I understood why the box factory existed—people need boxes. But in reality, the factory was a grift. Companies paid Bob to take their waste, and then paid him again to ship the good boxes back. He got paid twice for a single task!

Even then, the box factory wasn't that profitable. I found out that the company made a profit, but only just. When I was there it generated £23,000 on the bottom line (about $32,000). It was a miserable, marginal business, just scraping by. And yet, with a bit of imagination and some good management, it could have been so different.

BOB SLEPT THROUGH THE
GOLD RUSH OF THE 1990S

We have all heard the story about the people who got rich selling pickaxes during the Gold Rush, rather than panning for gold themselves.

There was a man who did this in real life. Samuel Brannan was born in 1819 and died in 1889. He literally sold pans, picks, and shovels to prospecting miners in San Francisco. He acquired pans for 20 cents each and sold them to miners for $15. He was the first actual millionaire of the Gold Rush. He got rich *before* the people trying to find the gold.

One hundred years later, at Bob's place, we had boxes.

It was the early 1990s, and the internet was in its infancy. You'd be forgiven for thinking that as our lives became increasingly digital, cardboard boxes would fade into the past, like carbon paper or typewriters.

In fact, the opposite happened.

As we all know, Amazon and a million other businesses transformed how we shop. Much of what shoppers buy now comes delivered through the mail. In the 1990s, packaging was about to become very important. *Big Cardboard* was about to enter a period of growth as prodigious as that of the internet itself.

At my old factory, our boxes were the most prosaic product imaginable: a floor, four walls, and a lid. But the internet totally changed what people needed from the humble box. If you look at

FBI investigate terrorism. This wasn't a theoretical debate about privacy versus security. People were dead. Alshamrani was dead, too—meaning that he had no privacy to protect. And the FBI had an obvious and reasonable interest in finding out whether he was acting alone or in concert with even more dangerous killers.

Apple took a huge risk with its reputation. It was condemned, repeatedly, by US Attorney Bill Barr for refusing to do what prosecutors wanted.

But this was an important battle for Apple because of the company's core principles around privacy. Apple treats privacy completely differently to most other digital companies.

The internet, and our mobile phones, are wonderful things. They have made our lives more convenient and more productive. But as we all know, that convenience has come at a great cost: Most of us have no privacy online. In particular, Google and Facebook have built a vast infrastructure around collecting your online data, and then selling that data to advertisers who use it to target you with ads online. Every app, login, service, and account you have online sucks data from you. The big tech companies know more about you than your family does.

Apple, however, has taken a different course. It generally discourages advertisers from targeting its users. It shields users' online data from other companies. Its internet browser, Safari, actively blocks advertisers. Apple's website says, "Privacy is a fundamental human right. At Apple, it's also one of our core values."

That's a *strong* statement: "Privacy is a fundamental human right."

Now you can see that when the FBI came calling, it was asking Apple to compromise its soul, one of the central differentiators between it and Facebook. In the short term, saying *no* made Apple unpopular.

But in the long run, Apple's sales only increased. Consumers understood the message: If you want a high-quality phone and more privacy online, then Apple is the company that takes this seriously.

WHICH IS BETTER, RYANAIR OR
BRITISH AIRWAYS?

The principle behind your business doesn't have to be a lofty, high-minded ideal (although it is nice when businesses think like that). Your principle can be purely practical.

Take air travel.

At first glance, Ryanair and British Airways both do the same thing. They are both airlines. But in fact they operate entirely different businesses.

British Airways made its fortune by dominating long-haul routes with huge airliners like the Boeing 747. London to New York. Paris to San Francisco. That kind of thing. They charge high prices for business-class seats with superb food.

But British Airways ignored small, obscure routes like Liverpool to Alicante, or Aarhus to Gdansk. British Airways' planes are too big. You can't make money flying a 747 (capacity: 700 passengers) in 90-minute hops. People balk at paying business-class prices for short flights.

So Ryanair filled in the gaps. The budget airline is based around a central logic: short routes, between less popular airports, with smaller planes. The routes that are uneconomical for British Airways.

Almost all of Ryanair's routes are within three hours of London and none of them cross the Atlantic. The Boeing 737 (capacity: about 200) makes up 95% of its fleet. That makes maintenance efficient and easier. They all take the same parts and require the same repairs. British Airways, by contrast, operates a dozen or more different types of jet and has all the maintenance complications that go with that.

These structural differences mean that most of the time, Ryanair and British Airways simply don't compete for the same passengers or even the same routes.

Because Ryanair flights are short, and because Ryanair doesn't bother with long-haul luxuries, the company will get you where you want to go very cheaply. Perhaps not in five-star comfort. But it won't cost you a lot.

Everything Ryanair does revolves around this central principle: cheap, short, and efficient. You might not find that principle inspiring, but that's not the point. The important thing is that Ryanair has a central organising logic that all its employees—and most of its customers—understand.

And that logic has paid huge dividends. Ryanair now serves more routes than any other airline on the planet, including British Airways.

GET READY TO TELL YOUR STORY AGAIN AND AGAIN

The takeaway is that Apple and Ryanair have something in common: Central, organising beliefs that make them qualitatively different to their competitors. Principles.

As a manager, you need to be able to articulate the principles on which your company is based to every employee and every customer. If you can't, you're sunk.

Your people will want to know what the big picture is. They want to hear your vision. And they want to hear it far more often than you'd think. On their first day at work; when you are setting expectations in a performance review; when you're launching a new project and want your staff to understand why it is important to succeed.

For individuals, there is a massive difference between just doing the job and knowing why your job is a crucial part of a larger plan.

The easiest way to see this in real life is to compare people playing soccer for fun in a park with professional footballers playing for high stakes in a Premier League stadium. In theory, it's the same game in both venues. But football played for fun is chaotic and messy. Even a team of talented amateurs can barely put three passes together. By contrast, professional players pass the ball accurately without looking, in the sure knowledge that their teammates will be in the right place at the right time to receive the ball. They can string together a chain of passes that count into the dozens. Obviously, professionals are better players than amateurs. Granted. But the teams that really succeed play to a system, a method of organization. Every player knows their individual role and how it fits into the bigger plan.

It's the same at work. Your principles should drive your vision, so that the motivation behind your plans is obvious. Everyone should know the plan. And everyone should know that *everyone else* knows the plan. So get ready to repeat yourself.

TEN-SECOND CHEAT SHEET

- The bedrock of your management should be about principle. You need a mission. Ethics. A difference you want to make. A higher calling. A vision of the future. Your staff and your customers need to know the big reason you show up at work every day.

- It cannot just be about the money.

- Everyone on your team should understand why your story is different to everyone else's.

- Everyone on your team should know why they are doing the job they are doing. They should not be doing it simply because that is the way it has always been done.

- Your principle can be lofty or political, if you are driven by ethics. It can be practical, if you are driven by superior product design. It can even be about value or prices, if the basis of your business is about saving your customers money.

- As a manager, you need to be able to articulate the principles on which your company stands to every employee and every customer, every day.

- Repetition doesn't spoil the prayer!

26

Strategy: How Amazon created Earth's greatest toy store and then burned it to the ground

STRATEGIC decisions are major choices that can affect the core of the company. But they differ from decisions of principle because they don't involve an existential challenge to your company's reason for being.

Strategic decisions are likely to require new investment and new staff; new risks and liabilities; new opportunities and new revenue.

Some examples:

- Whether to launch a new product.
- Whether to compete in a new geographic market.
- Whether to start a new line of research and development.

Like principle decisions, strategic decisions can make or break a company financially. But strategy is generally about a *part* of the company, whereas principle is about the company's *whole* existence.

Here is a particularly dramatic example, which went horribly wrong.

In April 2000 Amazon and Toys "R" Us made a joint

announcement that would reshape the world of toys. They were going into business together. All of Toys "R" Us's online sales would be handled exclusively by Amazon. On top of that, the only toys Amazon would sell would be from Toys "R" Us. All other toy retailers were banned from Amazon.

The scale of the alliance, and the speed at which it was built, were stunning. Instantly, the joint venture made it the No.1 online seller of toys on the planet. At a stroke, Walmart and Target—previously bigger toysellers than either company—found themselves locked out of Amazon and now running a distant third and fourth. The Amazon executive in charge of toys described it this way: "The main plan is that we're going to work together and create Earth's greatest toy store."

There were only advantages for both companies. Combined, Toys "R" Us and Amazon generated at least $12bn in toy sales that year. The deal increased Toys "R" Us's online sales tenfold as the years went by. Toys "R" Us's main digital-only rival was driven out of business within a year. And Amazon took a cut on every sale.

On paper, the alliance between Toys "R" Us and Amazon was one of the most brilliant retail strategies ever seen.

And yet the story ended in bankruptcy for Toys "R" Us.

After only three-and-a-half years, Toys "R" Us went to court to end the deal, furious at the way it was working out. Amazon paid Toys "R" Us $50m to go away. Toys "R" Us had to restart its web operations from scratch. The company staggered on but never really recovered. In 2017, Toys "R" Us declared itself broke and closed all its US stores.

What went wrong? Why did this obvious win-win crash so quickly?

It's worth going back to 1999, the year before the deal with Amazon, to see how desperate both companies were. Toys "R" Us's Christmas sales period in 1999 was an unmitigated public disaster. A rival company with a similar web address, eToys.com, had siphoned customers away from Toys "R" Us's official address,

Toys.com. That Christmas, Toys "R" Us sold less than $40m online. The other company, eToys.com, which had come from nowhere just a few months prior, sold $30m for the year—sales that might otherwise have gone to Toys "R" Us.

Worse, the Toys "R" Us site accepted orders from customers even though the company was unable to deliver them. When parents learned their kids' gifts would not arrive before Christmas Eve—thus disproving the existence of Santa Claus—they sued, generating ugly headlines.

So Toys "R" Us CEO John Eyler began casting about for alternatives. In January 2000, executives from Toys "R" Us and Amazon began talking to each other.

Amazon also experienced a terrible Christmas in 1999. The company sold $65m-worth of toys—not bad for a non-toy company. But Amazon lost $39m writing off unsold inventory because it had bought many more toys than it sold. When it came to toys, Amazon didn't know what it was doing, basically.

It turns out that selling toys is completely different from selling books, which was Amazon's primary expertise at the time. Books are an easy type of inventory to sell. They have a long shelf life (you can keep them for years if need be and classics remain relevant forever). They sell all year round. If no one buys them, publishers agree to take the inventory back and refund the retailer. With books, unsold inventory risk is extremely low.

With toys, the opposite is true. Roughly one-third of all toys are sold immediately before Christmas. If you don't sell a toy at Christmas, you are in for a long wait until the next customer comes along. There are few classics with toys—this year's hot game is next year's hula-hoop. Selling toys is a low-margin business precisely because of the risk involved in guessing, months ahead of time, what will sell. Suppliers absolutely will not take back unsold toys: No one wants them.

You can see why Toys "R" Us and Amazon were tempted to

get into bed together. With Toys' expertise and Amazon's online operational skills they would be unstoppable.

AN EARLY VICTORY AND A BACKUP PLAN

The Toys "R" Us section of Amazon.com was up and running by late September. The first Christmas went well. By the end of 2001, eToys.com, the pretender to the Toys.com throne, had been driven out of business. This was a significant victory. Back in 1999, Toys "R" Us's board of directors had considered doing a deal with eToys precisely because it was too much of a threat. Now eToys was gone.

But on the Amazon side, trouble was brewing. Its executives had noticed that Toys "R" Us struggled to keep toys in stock. Some toys just weren't available. Skateboards and videogames, for instance. Amazon began to realize that the exclusive aspect of the contract meant that Toys "R" Us could deliver far less than the full universe of toys Amazon expected, and not face competition.

Unbeknownst to Toys "R" Us, Amazon had a backup plan: The contract had a provision that said Toys "R" Us would have exclusivity on any toy it sold through Amazon. Thus any toy *not* being sold by Toys "R" Us was fair game, as far as Amazon was concerned.

In 2002 an Amazon executive wrote an internal memo describing the situation. "Amazon has effectively ceded control of the toy and baby stores to [Toys "R" Us]. This is not always a good thing," the memo said. The memo proposed that Amazon should start sourcing products from other companies if Toys "R" Us couldn't fill orders. Toys "R" Us "will be unhappy with any move we make," the memo said. That was a prediction that significantly understated the level of rage that followed.

Sure enough, in 2003 Toys "R" Us began to notice that rival

companies' products were showing up on Amazon.com. Even Target—Toys' archenemy—could be found selling games on Amazon. Toys "R" Us was furious that Amazon allowed competing toysellers to eat into its deal. Amazon countered that if Toys "R" Us didn't sell a toy, or if it was out of stock, then its exclusivity wasn't covered. Amazon could sell the toy via someone else.

The pact began to crumble into endless bickering over which products were allowed on Amazon and which were not. Toys "R" Us executives would see a rival product on the site and demand it be taken down. Amazon staff would either resist or comply, but shortly afterward another offending product would appear and the argument would start again.

Worse than that, Toys "R" Us still wasn't making money on its Amazon sales. Christmas 2003 was a record year, and Toys "R" Us recorded $376m in sales through Amazon. That's tenfold what it managed on its own website before the joint venture. Toys "R" Us should have celebrated that as a huge success. But behind the scenes, executives were unhappy. Toys "R" Us lost $18m to generate those sales.

WAR BREAKS OUT

In April 2004, Toys "R" Us discovered 4,000 toys on Amazon being sold by other vendors. Understandably, Toys "R" Us was livid. So it went to court.

The Amazon folks weren't livid. Rather, they thought the Toys "R" Us people were pathetic. During the litigation, a judge on the case remarked, "As an observation, all the Amazon employees are very condescending when they talk about [Toys "R" Us]."

Those executives later decided to spin the truth, the judge noted. The judge hinted that she did not trust Amazon founder

Jeff Bezos. "No doubt his knowledge and understanding went much deeper than revealed," she ruled.

Amazon lost the case, in 2006, and settled with Toys "R" Us.

The victory was an empty one. The original agreement in 2000 required Toys "R" Us to abandon its website completely—during the entire period, Toys.com had redirected to Amazon.com. By the latter half of the decade, Toys "R" Us had no online strategy of its own whatsoever. It had to start again from the beginning.

Half a decade of unprofitable sales with Amazon took its toll on Toys "R" Us. In 2005, Toys "R" Us did a leveraged buyout to obtain new cash to inject into the company. The deal involved an investment of $1.3bn, but the transaction was valued at $6.6bn. This left Toys "R" Us carrying over $5bn in loans. The payments hit $400 million per year. The new money came too late. Somehow, even though Toys "R" Us routinely booked $11bn in annual revenues, it couldn't carry the debt. The company filed for bankruptcy in 2017. (A new company later bought the name and reopened some of its stores.)

TWO CEOS COMPLETELY MISUNDERSTOOD EACH OTHER

There is a facile interpretation of all this: That Toys "R" Us failed to understand the importance of the internet, failed to adapt, and was driven under by the web.

That is not what happened.

The root of the failure can be traced to a meeting between the two companies' CEOs on June 28, 2000—before they signed their contract. Toys "R" Us's John Eyler flew to meet Amazon's Jeff Bezos at his Seattle headquarters specifically to discuss strategy, according to *The Wall Street Journal*.

Eyler explained to Bezos that the toy business revolves maniacally around a small minority of products, the hottest toys in any given year. About 1,500 toys fall into this category. There may be more than 40,000 toys for sale per year, but 97% of sales come from this top list, predominantly at Christmas. If you've got those bestsellers in stock, you'll be fine.

The challenge is that in January, no one knows what the hottest toy is going to be in December. Who the hell knows what kids will want 11 months from now? If you can make a good guess about how many toys you'll need for Christmas, and which specific toys will fall into the top 1,500 stock units, then you're a winner. The entire business is about instinct, experience, and prediction. At least, that is what Eyler told Bezos as he tried to get across to the Amazon founder that providing a relatively *limited* range of stock would be the key to their alliance.

Bezos had an entirely different philosophy. Amazon had been so successful with books because the site could provide any customer with any product at any time. The key to success was the *widest* assortment possible, Bezos believed. Bezos had chosen to go into business with Toys "R" Us precisely because the company had access to an almost unlimited range of toys.

Yet neither CEO fully realized during the conversation that he had fundamentally misunderstood the strategy of the other. Toys "R" Us thought it would be the exclusive toy provider to Amazon, thus allowing it to focus on only the top minority of toys. And Amazon thought it was gaining access to the vast range of toys that Toys "R" Us could supply.

That misunderstanding meant they went into the deal with mutually opposing strategies: limited versus unlimited; exclusive versus universal.

Somehow, neither noticed the chasm between them.

WHEN FAILURE IS COSTLY

There's a lot to unpick in the demise of the Amazon-Toys "R" Us alliance, strategy-wise. But the main thing to appreciate is that even though both companies' strategies were initially aligned, and they were both incentivized to make it work, the price of failure was high for both. Amazon poured millions into creating a special section of its site for Toys "R" Us. At one point 40% of all Amazon's warehouse space was devoted to Toys "R" Us merchandise. And of course, it had to pay $50m to extract itself from the deal.

It was even more costly for Toys "R" Us, of course. In addition to supplying the toys, the company agreed to pay Amazon $50m every year for its exclusive place on Amazon.com. It started each Christmas in the hole, in other words.

And while their incentives were aligned—they both wanted to sell as many toys as profitably as possible—their *disincentives* were diametrically antagonistic. Both sides were rewarded for their bad behavior. Toys "R" Us benefited by not providing a full universe of products; Amazon benefited by encroaching on Toys' exclusivity.

The big difference in terms of outcomes between the two companies was that for Toys "R" Us the stakes were much higher. The entirety of its online business was dependent on Amazon, a partner it belatedly discovered it did not control. A strategic decision can tank your whole company, if it's bad enough. For Amazon, the alliance was merely one category of business among myriad others. The failure of Amazon's Toys "R" Us strategy was bad—$50m-worth of bad—but Amazon was not fundamentally threatened by Toys' disappearance from its site.

Nonetheless the strategic fundamentals were the same for both sides:

- They tried to open up a whole new type of business.

- There was a lot at risk. Both companies staked a vast sum of money to develop the partnership.
- And there was no guarantee of success—failure would be costly.

When you're making a decision that contains those three signals, then the decision you are making is an important one *strategically*—and you'd better get it right. Given the high cost of failure for both Toys "R" Us and Amazon, it remains fascinating that they went into business with each other based on a mistake.

TEN-SECOND CHEAT SHEET

⌚ Strategic decisions can affect the core of the company but are not necessarily an existential challenge to your reason for being in business.

⌚ Strategic decisions typically involve trying to open up a new type of business such as launching a new product, competing in a new market, or starting a new line of research and development.

⌚ Strategic decisions require significant new investment or risk. Sometimes they can be big enough to make or break a company.

⌚ Often the cost of failure is high. So you need to get it right.

27

Tactics: Why trains actually do run on time

TACTICAL decisions are about incrementally moving the company forward. They are the most common decisions that managers make. Typical examples include:

- Whether to increase the ad budget.
- Whether to add a new salesperson to the team.
- Whether to respond to a false claim by a competitor in the media.

Tactical decisions are important but routine. Unlike decisions of strategy, they are not *bet the company* decisions. They are more about execution and improvement. They are about how you organize the management of your company internally, not about which markets your company is going to operate in.

MOST OF YOUR TIME WILL BE
SPENT ON TACTICS

It is tempting to conclude that tactical decisions are the least-important decisions. Indeed, some of them will be trivial. However, for managers, tactical decisions are the ones you will likely be making most frequently, every day, and they will be the ones that most often affect the people you supervise.

For your staff, tactical decisions will feel the most important because they will experience them most often. By contrast, decisions of strategy and principle will often seem distant and abstract to them. Most of your time will be spent on tactics.

As an example, here's a tactic I use to make sure all meetings run on time. Making your meetings start and finish on time may seem trivial. But if you have ever worked for an organization where meetings persistently run late, you'll know how disheartening it can become.

HOW TO MAKE SURE NO ONE IS EVER LATE FOR A MEETING

Meetings are the curse of management. The more senior a manager you become, the more meetings you are likely to have. At the top level of companies—the CEO level—the work that managers do consists almost entirely of meetings.

Having lots of meetings on your daily calendar presents a logistical problem. If one meeting starts late, it is likely to end late too. That will make you late for the next meeting. And if that meeting runs late, your entire schedule starts to topple like dominoes as one meeting's tardiness pushes into the next.

The reason this happens is because meetings have a weak link. They are often delayed while staff wait for everyone to be there. This, by definition, means that meetings are only as punctual as the least-punctual person on your team.

Think about that. It's crazy. Why would you run a race at the pace of the slowest runner on the squad?

In fact, there are two famous companies that notoriously did run their meetings at the speed of the slowest runner on the squad: Google and Yahoo!

Yahoo! CEO Marissa Mayer's worst habit

The most extreme example of bad meetings management I ever encountered involves Marissa Mayer, the former CEO of Yahoo!, who was previously a senior executive at Google.

At both companies she notoriously let one meeting run into the next. By the afternoon, her schedule would often be hours late. People would sit outside her office for ages, waiting for her to get done with her previous meeting, their own calendars now in tatters.

A Yahoo! executive once told one of my colleagues: "There has not been a single meeting or event here that since she has taken the helm she arrives on time—not one."

"The amount of wasted time and anger building up from her lack of caring or understanding that it isn't just her time that matters is astounding. She is routinely over an hour late for things," the source told him.

Her lateness became legendary across Silicon Valley. According to the book *Marissa Mayer and the Fight to Save Yahoo!*, Mayer was once two hours late for a dinner with the CEOs of Unilever and Interpublic Group—two huge advertising clients which control budgets worth billions. She had fallen asleep in her hotel room at the Cannes advertising festival, an important conference for online media. (In Mayer's defense, she was jetlagged after a long flight from California to France.)

Bad managers tend not to tackle the late meeting problem because there is no immediate cost to being five minutes late. But what if you are running a business—like a restaurant or theater—where routinely being late is fatal?

Trains mostly don't run late

In London I once got the train out of Paddington station to go to Oxford. I was ten minutes early, so I had plenty of time to settle into my seat and arrange my sandwiches, bag of crisps, and can of pre-mixed gin and tonic from Marks & Spencer on the table in front of me. As is tradition.

Before the train left, I looked out of the window and noticed that a man and a woman who had arrived on time couldn't open the door to the carriage. The conductor had locked the train doors *before* the scheduled departure.

Seconds later the train pulled away, leaving the furious couple stranded on the platform. They had arrived exactly on time for the train. But *exactly on time* turns out to be too late for a train out of London.

In the UK train companies have a rule: Passengers must get on the train 30 seconds before the train is scheduled to leave. Then the doors are locked. And then the train is guaranteed to leave on time. (I know everyone complains about trains in Britain being persistently late, but statistics show that about 90% of UK trains actually do set off on time!) The point is that if you are 30 seconds too late for a train in Britain, it leaves without you.

That sucks for you.

But it is great for the vast majority of passengers who have their shit together and want to leave on time.

It's also great for the train companies. Because you absolutely cannot run a railroad if you're only moving at the pace of the slowest passenger on the platform.

The train leaves the station whether the passengers are ready or not

So I recommend you use a rule for meetings with your team. The rule is called: "The train leaves the station whether the passengers are ready or not." Meetings should start on time even if some of you are running late. Even if the most important person in the meeting— your boss—is running late, start the meeting without him or her.

And encourage your staff to start without *you* if you are late.

Guess what? It works. Meetings start on time. Folks attending them are incentivized to end them on time, too, because no one wants to miss the next one. And if you miss a meeting, no one cares. There should be no punishment for being late, other than you will have missed the information at the beginning of the meeting.

Your company will survive if you are five minutes late to a meeting. (And if it can't, then that's a bad sign!)

My "The train leaves the station whether the passengers are ready or not" rule is, obviously, a mere tactic—it's a device that helps you move quickly. It's not a strategy—there is no financial or risk consequence to scheduling a meeting. It's not a principle—the soul of the company isn't about meetings. That would be ridiculous.

It is an incremental improvement that will keep your company moving fast.

TEN-SECOND CHEAT SHEET

- Tactical decisions are about incrementally moving the company forward. They are the most common decisions that managers make.

- Tactical decisions are the ones that most frequently affect the people you supervise directly.

- For them, tactical decisions will feel the most important because they will experience them most often. Decisions of principle and strategy have bigger stakes but will feel more distant to frontline workers.

- Want to make all your meetings run on time? Tell your staff that "The train leaves the station whether the passengers are ready or not."

28

Category errors: The art of getting it wrong

THIS is all very easily said, but in real life problems do not come along ready-labeled as decisions of principle, strategy, or tactics. You have to carefully figure that out yourself.

It is important to know which type of decision you are making when you make it. Because this is something you can easily get wrong. Sometimes important decisions of principle disguise themselves as strategic or tactical problems. It is easy to make a category error by thinking you are solving a tactical problem, when in reality it's a decision of strategy or principle. Problems don't announce which category they are in, so think carefully. Being able to detect that trap is crucial.

This is a good way to test what type of problem you are faced with:

- **Tactical errors** can be corrected quickly. If you make one, no one will lose their job.
- **Strategic errors** are likely to cost a lot of money. They can *potentially* threaten the whole company. And they *might* cost you your job.

- **Errors of principle** are *highly likely* to cost you or others your jobs, and may bankrupt the whole company or forever tarnish your brand.

WHAT IF APPLE HAD MADE A CATEGORY ERROR WITH THE FBI?

Let's go back to the story of Apple vs. the FBI. Clearly, Apple treated the FBI's requests to open the killers' phones as a matter of principle—something that went against the fundamental basis of the company, preventing them from cooperating.

But a lesser company, under the same circumstances, could have seen the decision as a matter of strategy: For instance, Apple could have decided that the FBI's request was mostly a threat to their revenues. If they opened the phones, Apple might lose customers who care about privacy and security. The strategic decision would have been to oppose the FBI in order to safeguard those revenues.

Of course, that would have been a lousy decision. Eventually, someone would have figured out that Apple wasn't opposing the FBI because important ethics were at stake, but rather because they just wanted the money. And that would have made Apple look cheap and cynical, and hurt its brand.

It is also possible that Apple might have seen the FBI as a tactical problem. It is easy to imagine Apple's PR team concluding that opposing a terrorism investigation could generate terrible headlines. Maybe the company should just give up and do what the FBI says—and hope it all goes away.

But that too would have been a lousy decision. Eventually someone would realize that Apple's rhetoric about privacy was bogus, and that they had created a hackable backdoor into a phone they were promoting as secure. The headlines might have been even worse again.

TEN-SECOND CHEAT SHEET

🕑 Managers make three types of decisions: decisions of principle, decisions of strategy, and decisions of tactics.

🕑 It is important to know which type of decision you are making, because the cost of making an error is different within each category.

🕑 You can usually make a tactical error and reverse course with minimal difficulty.

🕑 Strategic errors likely come at a high cost.

🕑 Errors of principle will threaten your entire vision and credibility.

🕑 Making a category error—thinking you are making one type of decision when in fact it is another—is an especially good way to generate a catastrophe.

THAT'S IT

That's it. That's everything useful I know about how to manage people. I hope you found it helpful. Not all my advice will be relevant to every situation or every job, obviously. So use your judgment.

And good luck. You'll need it!

If, at this final stage, you are still harboring the fantasy of behaving like a Hollywood Boss who yells at their underlings and fires people on a whim, consider what Steve Brill told me as I was writing this book. You may remember from the first chapter that Brill was the guy who sent a mean email about my writing to the entire office.

He now cringes at the memory of being *that guy*. He has since made efforts to change.

"It would indeed be a classic example of stupid, impulsive, terrible management," he told me when I reminded him about it. "Frustration about the quality of work—whether justified or not—should never be an excuse for embarrassing someone publicly."

"I used to respond to queries like this by saying that those incidents were all about the quality of our product, not about whether someone didn't get me a cup of coffee fast enough. But that's not enough. Beyond being unfair, it's counterproductive because it fosters fear. And it doesn't make for a great recruiting story—something I pride myself on," he said. "If you don't get better at something—in this case, management and training—after you do it for decades, that would be pretty bad."

There you have it. Even Hollywood Bosses ultimately regret what they do.

(Brill isn't compromising on the issue of whether he bit Jim Cramer in a swimming pool, by the way: "I still maintain that Jim made that up, but whatever.")

I said at the beginning of the book that every chapter would include a bullet-point summary, just in case you don't have time to read the whole thing. So here is a cheat-sheet for the entire book.

TEN-SECOND CHEAT SHEET

- If someone does some work for you, say "thank you." Say "thank you" for everything.

- Have a plan. Better yet, turn their plan into your plan.

- Good hiring will solve 80% of your problems. You should prioritize hiring new talent above almost any other managerial task.

- Every new hire should increase the average talent level of the team.

- Win the war on mushroom farming: Don't bullshit your staff. Workers want their bosses to be clear about the task in front of them. Be transparent.

- Change is better than unemployment. Be straightforward with your colleagues about what change will entail. It's worth describing the big picture so that everyone understands the nature of the business you are in and what is at stake.

- Repetition doesn't spoil the prayer: The basis of good

communication is repetition, and you will need to use all the communication channels available to you.

⌚ Prioritize & delete: Keep your team focused on the most important tasks by routinely deleting the more trivial jobs from their to-do lists.

⌚ Use the whales & fails method to get staff thinking about why they succeeded or why they failed. Learn from both.

⌚ Praise success when you see it. Use examples of success to generate new ideas about other types of work, products, or services that might also be successful.

⌚ Continuously applying the whales & fails method will mechanically move up both the average performance of your team and the total results they get without requiring any extra work, skill or staff. Consistency is the hobgoblin of excellence.

⌚ Use the incredible power of being slightly better than average. Stop people from working on underperforming tasks and move those staff members to more productive tasks.

⌚ You are floating in an ocean of constant improvement, and your boats are being borne forward by that. New ideas generate growth, and people tend to become better at their jobs over time. These two dynamics will help you generate compounding gains in performance over the long term.

⌚ Work is not a popularity contest. It is a getting-things-done contest. Judge staff on the quality of their work, not whether they talk a good game.

⌚ Solve the strip-club problem with data. Don't manage

by anecdote. Use data that is tangible, measurable, and checkable.

- Beware of the quant fallacy: There's a difference between having good data and applying judgment to good data. Don't outsource your judgment to the data.

- Remember the rule of five: Teams with six or more members will approach the threshold of dysfunction.

- Managing up is a highly undervalued skill. Promote people who exhibit level four behavior. (And use the Van Halen test to avoid promoting people who cannot follow instructions.)

- Nip trouble in the bud. Problems don't go away on their own. Step in quickly to resolve them.

- If your staff believe that the only reason to come to work is for the money, then you are probably a bad manager.

- Managers make three types of decisions based on principles, strategy, or tactics.

- You can usually make a tactical error and reverse course with minimum difficulty. Strategic errors likely come at a high cost. Errors of principle will threaten your entire vision and credibility.

- Making a category error—thinking you are making one type of decision when in fact it is another—is an especially good way to generate a catastrophe.

THANK YOU

Acknowledgements

I have a lot of people to thank for the help they gave me while I wrote this book.

First, Philippa Stock, for her patience and support while I wrote the manuscript. Christopher Parker at Harriman House for his incredibly helpful guidance on the preparation of this book.

The editors with whom I have worked over the last ten years are the ones from whom I have learned the most. Their fierce competitiveness has built a formidable organization that for a long time was consistently underestimated by the rest of the world. I am also grateful to all my colleagues—there have been hundreds—who tolerated being the unwitting test-subjects for my obsession with whales & fails, and other material in this book.

Thank you.

INDEX

ABOUT THE AUTHOR

JIM EDWARDS is the former editor-in-chief of Insider's news division and was the founding editor of *Business Insider* UK. He has also been a managing editor at Adweek, and a Knight-Bagehot Fellow at the Columbia Business School.

His work has appeared in *Slate*, *Salon*, *The Independent*, *The Nation* and on AOL and MTV. He won the Neal award for business journalism in 2005 for a series investigating bribes and kickbacks in the advertising business.

If you have feedback for the author or questions about this book, please get in touch at saythankyouforeverything@gmail.com.

CPSIA information can be obtained
at www.ICGtesting.com
Printed in the USA
JSHW032114070423
39987JS00005B/17